CAMBRIDGE MUSIC HANDBOOKS

Chopin: The Piano Concertos

CAMBRIDGE MUSIC HANDBOOKS

GENERAL EDITOR   Julian Rushton

Published titles

Chopin: The Piano Concertos

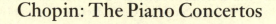

John Rink

Royal Holloway, University of London

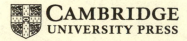

CAMBRIDGE
UNIVERSITY PRESS

Published by the Press Syndicate of the University of Cambridge
The Pitt Building, Trumpington Street, Cambridge CB2 1RP, United Kingdom

Cambridge University Press
The Edinburgh Building, Cambridge CB2 2RU, United Kingdom
40 West 20th Street, New York, NY 10011–4211, USA
10 Stamford Road, Oakleigh, Melbourne 3166, Australia

First published 1997

Printed in the United Kingdom at the University Press, Cambridge

Typeset in Ehrhardt MT 10½/13pt, in Quark Xpress™ [SE]

A catalogue record for this book is available from the British Library

Library of Congress cataloguing in publication data
Rink, John.
Chopin: The Piano Concertos / John Rink.
p.   cm. – (Cambridge music handbooks)
Discography
Includes bibliographical references and index.
ISBN 0 521 44109 9 (hardback) – ISBN 0 521 44660 0 (paperback)
1. Chopin, Frédéric, 1810–1849.   Concertos, piano, orchestra.
2. Concertos (Piano) – Analysis, appreciation.   I. Title.
II. Series.
ML410.C54RR54   1997
784.2′62′092–dc21   97–6905   CIP

ISBN 0 521 44109 9 hardback
ISBN 0 521 44660 0 paperback

to Jean-Jacques Eigeldinger and Jim Samson
with thanks

Contents

Contents

Preface

Chopin's piano concertos have enjoyed enormous popularity ever since their composition in 1829–30, but they have also suffered some of the harshest scholarly criticism inflicted on his works. Intended to launch his career as a composer-pianist, the concertos have typically been regarded in the literature as juvenilia inferior to his mature masterpieces. Nevertheless, when viewed as music to be performed rather than scores to be dissected on paper, they belong to his most successful creations, capable of evoking profound emotion in listener and pianist alike, and representative of an altogether unique, innovative pianism to be fully exploited in the composer's later music.

This handbook attempts to set the record straight, re-evaluating the concertos against the early nineteenth-century traditions that shaped them so that their many outstanding qualities can be better appreciated. After establishing such a background in Chapter 1, I describe the genesis of the two concertos, trace the history of Chopin's first and subsequent performances, and discuss his use of the concertos as teaching pieces in Chapter 2. An extended investigation of the critical, editorial and inter-pretative reception of the two works follows in Chapter 3, highlighting the contrast between initial reactions and the censure of later writers.

The fourth chapter presents an analysis based on performance-related criteria. For each movement a formal outline is provided, but the principal analytical focus is on the music's temporal shaping and the role of 'musical gesture' in creating the powerful effect alluded to above. In a sense this study provides a rationale for the most commonly criticised elements of the two pieces – which work well in performance, however idiosyncratic they appear in the score. My aim throughout is to redress the anachronistic and tendentious criticisms of past authors, as it were justifying through late twentieth-century analytical description the enthusiastic reception of the two works in the first half of the nineteenth century. This same rehabilitation is attempted in the final chapter on the *Allegro de concert* Op. 46, Chopin's enigmatic 'third concerto'.

A few practical comments will assist readers. Sources cited more than once are referred to by short title in the notes; the select bibliography provides full details in such cases. References to the concertos before publication are distinguished by key, whereas opus numbers designate the published works. (As the concertos appeared in reverse chronological order, 'No. 1' and 'No. 2' are avoided to prevent confusion.) Careted numerals represent scale degrees; lower-case Roman numerals denote minor harmonies, upper-case major ones. Pitch classes are indicated by capital letters, whereas the Helmholtz system specifies pitch register when necessary. Readers are advised to consult Jan Ekier's edition of Op. 21 issued by Polskie Wydawnictwo Muzyczne in the Polskie Wydanie Narodowe (Polish National Edition), and Ewald Zimmermann's of Op. 11 published by Henle Verlag. Neither is without problems, nor are they true Urtexts, but at present they are the best available. The forthcoming volume of the concertos in *The Complete Chopin – A New Critical Edition*, published by Peters Edition London, will soon provide an alternative to both.

This book has benefited enormously from the assistance of Jean-Jacques Eigeldinger and Jim Samson, whose outstanding research and generosity of spirit have proved invaluable to me throughout this project and in other pursuits. I should also like to thank David Charlton, Ruth Darton, Katharine Ellis, Christophe Grabowski, Jeffrey Kallberg, Michał Kubicki, Antonina Machowska, Jürgen Neubacher, Stephen O'Hanlon, Lucy Passmore and Hanna Wróblewska-Straus. Finally, I am grateful to the Music Department, Royal Holloway, University of London for financial support, and to Julian Rushton, Penny Souster and the production team at Cambridge University Press for their patience and wisdom.

I

Contexts

The early nineteenth-century piano concerto

The fundamental upheavals in politics and culture that rocked Europe during the late eighteenth and early nineteenth centuries radically altered musical practice and the institutions that supported it. New instrumental and vocal genres, a burgeoning concert and operatic industry, and an entire class of 'professional performers' rapidly evolved alongside countless music-publishing and instrument-building ventures, all aiming to satisfy the demands of a bourgeoisie revelling in its recently acquired power as patrons of the arts. The piano was at the heart of this expanding musical world, especially in Vienna, which boasted eminent figures like Mozart, Beethoven, Ries, Hummel and Moscheles, and, later, in Paris, to which dozens of keyboard virtuosos flocked each year 'like swarms of locusts', in Heine's memorable phrase. Continual advances in piano design and construction enabled keyboardists to attain new heights of technical brilliance on both the lighter Viennese and the more sonorous English pianos, and sparkle and dexterity were further enhanced by Erard's double escapement action, patented in 1821. Such improvements also facilitated the piano's penetration into the middle-class home, providing composer-pianists with sizeable amateur markets demanding tailormade pieces or simplifications of the virtuoso *tours de force* heard in the concert hall.

By the time Paris had established itself in the 1830s as 'capital of the nineteenth century',[1] keyboard virtuosity and the operatic stage completely dominated professional music-making, much to the chagrin of critics like Schumann, who lamented the damage thus inflicted on 'serious' compositional activity.[2] But even he recognised the charm and appeal of the best virtuoso music, not all of which is the cliché-ridden, meretricious claptrap habitually derided by scholars. Early nineteenth-century keyboard virtuosity has in fact unjustly acquired a poisonous reputation (in contrast to the term's original associations with worth and excellence):[3] keyboard virtuosos wielded enormous power over audiences through their exultant technical displays, and some of the finest gave concerts attended by the young Chopin in 1820s Warsaw.

Composer-pianists like these played largely their own music, written not for posterity but for immediate consumption in a particular season. Most churned out a seemingly inexhaustible supply of concertos, rondos, variations, potpourris and fantasies (usually on operatic arias), as well as the improvisations that would typically end their smorgasbord-like benefit concerts.[4] Of these various genres, the concerto suffered changes in fashion more than others, and its relatively lofty nature restricted the amateur market for published concertos. Nevertheless, a large corpus of virtuoso concertos survives to this day, alongside the 'symphonic concertos' of Beethoven, notably Op. 61 for violin and Nos. 3–5 for piano, which belong to a tradition stemming from Mozart's K. 466 and ultimately linked to Liszt's and Brahms's later concertos.[5] Inspired in different ways by Beethoven, and drawing upon an earlier keyboard idiom manifest most transparently in Mozart's K. 537, virtuoso concertos straddled two domains, those of 'serious' art music and 'popular' concert music. The strategy in most was to minimise the orchestra's role, in part for practical reasons, as they had to be performable as solos or with quartet or quintet accompaniment, depending upon available forces on a given occasion. Thus the principle of contrast so basic to the genre was assimilated into the piano part itself.[6]

Throughout the concerto's lengthy history, the principle of contrast has had many incarnations. Writers in the mid eighteenth century defined it in terms of textural oppositions (ripieno/concertino, ritornello/solo), while later theorists such as Vogler and Koch referred more to harmonic polarities. Even later ones – among them Czerny and Prout – focused on thematic oppositions, as in the 'double exposition form' that became the putative, if anachronistic, norm of classical concerto design.[7] For all its problems, Czerny's model is the one most applicable to Chopin's concertos and many virtuoso specimens, namely, four tutti sections interspersed with three lengthy solo sections that correspond to the ternary components of mid nineteenth-century sonata form (see

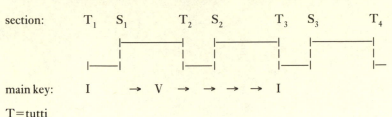

Figure 1.1 Czerny's model of first-movement concerto form
(from Stevens, 'Theme', 48)

Figure 1.1). As Jane Stevens writes, these tuttis had all but lost their ritornello function by Czerny's time: 'Although the first tutti retains the character of a long, expositionlike section, the other three tuttis are reduced in importance' – especially in articulating the standard tonal plan, which involves a modulation to the dominant or another key within the first solo and an eventual return to the tonic after a retransition (culminatory build-up in V) at the end of the second solo. Stevens concludes that Czerny's model diminishes 'both the role of the orchestra and the formal significance of textural contrast', placing 'increased importance on melody as a leading determinant of form'.[8] In this respect at least, it accurately reflects the design of most early nineteenth-century virtuoso concertos, which – like many works in the *stile brillante* – thrived on often abrupt alternations between 'poetry' and 'display' (Jim Samson's terms)[9] or, more specifically, between 'stable' thematic statements and discursive passagework, in the 'two-phase construction' defined by Józef Chomiński.[10]

The principle of alternation shaped not only virtuoso concertos but other early nineteenth-century music – for instance, Grand Opera,[11] which, like the concerto, fostered soloistic technical brilliance, the portrayal of 'characters' and 'moods', and a certain 'heart-on-sleeve emotionalism'.[12] Evidence of the unusually close relation between these genres can be seen in the cadenzas and recitatives of many concertos. Although after Beethoven's time cadenzas started disappearing from the virtuoso concerto (they were hardly necessary, given the almost ubiquitous bravura writing), recitatives increased in importance in concertos like Moscheles' G minor and Chopin's F minor, which recall earlier

sonata-form analogue:	----	exposition			development		recapitulation		coda
thematic group/ section:		theme 1	*Spiel-episode* 1	theme 2	*Spiel-episode* 2	new theme?	virtuosity	theme 1	*Spiel-episode* 3	theme 2	'finale'
tutti/solo:	T_1	S_1		T_2	S_2			T_3	S_3		T_4
main key:	I	----$\longrightarrow$	new key (e.g. III, V)		----$\longrightarrow$ V	I				

Figure 1.2 Archetypal virtuoso concerto first movement

examples like Mozart's K. 271. Melodic types in both solos and tuttis also betray opera's influence, even in Chopin's *Allegro de concert*, written as the virtuoso era was drawing to a close and the tasks of composer and performer-as-interpreter becoming more distinct.

As a young man, Chopin had ample contact with the parallel worlds of opera and keyboard virtuosity. For instance, he performed concertos by Gyrowetz, Ries, Hummel, Moscheles, Kalkbrenner, and, possibly, Weber and Field, and later he would also encounter the concertos of (among others) Dussek, Spohr, Steibelt, Cramer, Döhler, Herz, Pixis and Klengel,[13] thus gaining exposure to a concerto idiom that can readily be characterised in terms of the alternation between theme and passagework described above.

The striking consistency of the virtuoso concerto has been demonstrated in an exhaustive study by Isabella Amster,[14] who discerns a recurrent first-movement pattern accommodating numerous variants but in each case commencing with a tutti that establishes the principal themes in preparation for the first solo. This either restates the main and secondary themes in a virtuosically heightened style or replaces them with new 'brilliant' themes. Indeed, virtuosity dominates the first solo (contrary to the sonata form's usual balance), in a progression from the initial theme(s) through a bravura *Spielepisode* that modulates to a new key, then the typically contrasting second theme and finally a second *Spielepisode* (see Figure 1.2). After the second tutti comes one or more of the following: a new solo theme, usually long-breathed and richly embellished; a virtuosic development of exposition material analogous to the first and second *Spielepisoden*; an independent, non-developmental section; the recapitulation itself. Whatever its point of origin, the reprise stays close to the exposition apart from minor adjustments (occasionally the first *Spielepisode* or one of the themes is omitted), except that the second *Spielepisode* is generally replaced by a stirring conclusion designed to build excitement – comparable in effect to an operatic finale[15] or, on a smaller scale, a cabaletta. The ensuing slow movement, with its limited opportunities for display, tends to be perfunctory, although there is music of great beauty in the three most important influences on Chopin's concertos – Hummel's A minor Op. 85, Kalkbrenner's D minor Op. 61 and Moscheles' G minor Op. 58. The third movement is almost always a rondo structurally similar to those of

Mozart and Beethoven, although, as in the first movement, the virtuosic element is embodied in extended sections of passagework sandwiched between themes, with an especially brilliant 'finale' after the last thematic statement. Many are coloured by national idioms, as are Chopin's independent *Rondo à la mazur* Op. 5 and *Rondo à la krakowiak* Op. 14.

Amster notes that the 'brilliant' figuration within the virtuoso concerto generally includes scales, either unembellished (diatonic; chromatic; in thirds, sixths or tenths) or varied (with appoggiaturas, reaching-over notes, anticipations, etc.); arpeggios; repeated-note figures; *Rollfiguren* (in which one note remains fixed while other parts move); octaves; leaps; and patterns in thirds, fourths, fifths and sixths, used alone or with other configurations. As mentioned above, the orchestral accompaniment receives little weight, the spotlight instead firmly fixed on the soloist.

As we shall see, some of this template applies to Chopin's F minor and E minor Concertos but by no means all. Chopin's own remarks indicate an effort to achieve something out of the ordinary, as does comparison with his earlier music, much of which bears a closer relation to its models than do Op. 11 and Op. 21, notwithstanding the astonishing originality apparent from very early on.

Chopin's early music

Chopin's first extant compositions are the G minor and B♭ major Polonaises from 1817, both impressive as the work of a seven-year-old but not really distinct from the contemporary polonaises of Ogiński and others, and certainly a far cry from his first mature polonaises, Op. 26 Nos. 1 and 2, written in Paris in 1835 after a fundamental rethinking of the genre. In the meantime, Chopin had completed his 'apprenticeship' in Warsaw and had established himself in the French capital after an unsuccessful eight-month sojourn in Vienna designed as the springboard of his virtuoso career. This was an intensely traumatic time for him and his native Poland, following the brutally suppressed Warsaw Uprising of November 1830 and the state of siege that prevailed until August 1831, just before he arrived in Paris.

Poland had in contrast enjoyed a period of relative stability throughout Chopin's youth, after the creation in 1815 of a kingdom ruled by the

Russian tsar Alexander I. During this time both the sciences and the arts flourished, and new educational institutions and societies were founded.[16] Music publishing grew rapidly here as elsewhere, initially under the aegis of Chopin's composition teacher Józef Elsner, and during the 1820s Polish editions of piano works by Hummel, Field, Ries and others could be bought in Warsaw shops, in addition to piano arrangements of operas by Rossini, Weber, Auber and Boïeldieu – many of them performed at the Teatr Narodowy (National Theatre) under the directorship of Karol Kurpiński, and heard by Chopin. There were also imported scores of Haydn, Mozart and, to a limited extent, Beethoven.[17] By no means a provincial backwater, Warsaw played host to many touring virtuosos and singers, among others Hummel, Szymanowska, Catalani, Sontag and Paganini,[18] all of whom fed Chopin's growing appetite for a career as composer-pianist, directly or indirectly inspiring virtuoso compositions such as his four solo rondos, 'Là ci darem' Variations, *Fantasy on Polish Airs*, *Rondo à la krakowiak* and concertos. These were the key works in his portfolio when he left Warsaw for Vienna on 2 November 1830.

Chopin's education in Warsaw was not entirely conventional, particularly his keyboard training. His first teacher, Adalbert (Wojciech) Żywny, was himself a violinist, but he laid the groundwork of Chopin's keyboard technique as well as his lifelong love of Bach and Mozart, two stylistic influences of the utmost importance.[19] Although he later had guidance from Wilhelm Würfel, a distinguished pianist and organist, Chopin essentially taught himself to play; the result was an idiosyncratic keyboard style based on the beauty of sound, nuance, legato *cantabile*, suppleness, simplicity and colouristic variety.[20]

Chopin's composition training was more rigorous, initial advice from Żywny leading to private lessons with Elsner and then formal enrolment at the Szkoła Główna Muzyki (Central School of Music), where he received a solid grounding in counterpoint, thoroughbass, rhetoric and aesthetics, taught largely by means of eighteenth-century theoretical texts.[21] To some extent Elsner indulged his young pupil's genius, absolving him from certain exercises required of such colleagues as Tomasz Nidecki and Ignacy Feliks Dobrzyński (who feature later in this book). But he did insist upon the acquisition of orchestration technique[22] and the mastery of compositional form. Elsner's own music reveals an innovative if orthodox use of the Viennese sonata principle, suggesting that some of the structural anomalies in Chopin's Warsaw-period compositions – not least the E minor Concerto – should be understood as calculated experiments sanctioned by a skilled and knowledgeable teacher.

However rich Warsaw's cultural life might have been, it could not compete with centres like Berlin (which Chopin visited in September 1828, hearing operas by Spontini, Cimarosa, Onslow, Weber and Winter, as well as Handel's 'Ode to St Cecilia') or Vienna, Europe's musical capital at the time. Chopin's first trip to Vienna, in August 1829, was an unqualified success (unlike his second, extended stay there from November 1830 to July 1831). He gave two concerts featuring his 'Là ci darem' Variations and *Rondo à la krakowiak* as well as improvisations on Boïeldieu's *La Dame blanche* and the Polish folksong 'Chmiel', and he earned a rapturous response from a notoriously reticent audience. One reviewer commented: 'From the style of his playing as well as the characteristics of his compositions one may already detect a spark of genius, at least in regard to his unique forms and striking individuality.'[23]

Improvisations on national melodies were hardly unusual for early nineteenth-century virtuoso pianists, but in Chopin's case they represent an affinity with folk idioms that would bear particular fruit in his mazurkas and waltzes as well as the two concertos, fostered on various summer excursions from Warsaw to Szafarnia, where he encountered 'rustic' songs and dances such as the mazur, the lively oberek and the more reflective kujawiak. In Warsaw, he had already gained exposure to the polonaise, a processional dance of aristocratic pedigree, as the G minor and B♭ major pieces from 1817 bear witness.

Chopin's early music reflects in varying degrees the influences identified above – opera (especially Rossinian *bel canto*), virtuoso pianism (particularly that of Hummel, Weber and Field), national idioms (whether rural or urban), eighteenth-century masters (Bach and Mozart above all) and improvisation. The latter's role in defining Chopin's style should not be underestimated: not only did he compose at the piano, carefully crafting individual passages before committing them to paper, but he was expert at improvising in public concerts and the more private salons where he made a home for himself in 1830s and 1840s Paris.[24]

Although the works composed before and immediately after his arrival in Paris can be variously grouped, the following categories are helpful if not watertight:

a.   'private' works based on classical archetypes (Sonata in C minor Op. 4 and Trio in G minor Op. 8)
b.   smaller genres, intended largely for private performance (polonaises, mazurkas, waltzes, écossaises, études, nocturnes, songs, etc.)
c.   'post-classical concert music'[25] in the *stile brillante* (Rondo in C minor Op. 1, 'Là ci darem' Variations Op. 2, *Polonaise brillante* Op. 3, *Rondo à la mazur* Op. 5, *Fantasy on Polish Airs* Op. 13, *Rondo à la krakowiak* Op. 14, Rondo in E♭ major Op. 16, *Grande polonaise* Op. 22, Rondo in C major Op. 73, Variations on 'Der Schweizerbub' and the two concertos).[26]

It must be stressed that the concertos stand out in their class despite shared characteristics, or at least signs of lessons learnt in composing earlier 'brilliant' pieces. Except for the variation sets, Chopin's music in the *stile brillante* tends to maintain the strict alternation between theme and bravura passagework described earlier, with the effect a rather eclectic blend of sometimes incompatible materials, although gradually he succeeded in achieving greater synthesis between such sections, particularly in music from the late 1820s onwards.[27] The more stylistically accomplished repertoire from the period also displays a manipulation of impulse lacking in previous works: built upon a seemingly endless succession of sequential patterns clothed in all manner of virtuoso finery, the passagework in Chopin's first 'brilliant' pieces has little innate direction, any forward propulsion being further stifled by a leaden phrase rhythm, that is, the larger accentual patterns set up by four- and eight-bar units, among others. Greater control of momentum can be seen, however, in the 'finale' to Op. 13 and the episodic material in Op. 14, although in both cases the figuration itself sounds derivative and less 'natural' in shaping and inner impulse than that of the two concertos, the virtuosity of which not only assumes an expressive role but also reflects the suppleness and facility at the heart of Chopin's keyboard technique.

The introductions to Op. 13 and Op. 14, in contrast, contain some of Chopin's most original writing yet, likewise the introduction to Op. 2, each pointing in different ways to what would follow in the concertos. Another anticipation occurs in the middle section of the *Grande polonaise* Op. 22, its sequential 'announcements' in octaves analogous to gestures in the concertos' third movements. Additional commonalities include the use of 'finales' – in Opp. 5, 16, 22, 73 – to generate a last burst of energy (a feature heralding Chopin's heightened sensitivity to closure, evident in both the increasing concentration of structural weight towards the end of pieces, sometimes in extended structural cadences within foreshortened reprises, and the enhanced role of codas in ensuring large-scale proportion) and harmonic audacities such as parallel diminished sevenths or discursive right-hand chromaticism over left-hand pedal points.

As for tonal schemes, the concertos draw principally from music in the first and second groups above rather than the 'brilliant' compositions. The unorthodox structures in the first movements of the Sonata and the Trio are one obvious precursor. Both have monotonal expositions and recapitulations centred on harmonies other than the tonic (in violation of classical norms): Op. 4's reprise starts in B♭ minor, not C minor, and in Op. 8 the second subject returns in the minor dominant. These 'infringements', like the tonal idiosyncrasies of the concertos' first movements, have been attributed to ignorance of the Viennese sonata principle on the part of Warsaw composers, whereas they may simply represent the experimentation referred to earlier, undertaken with more or less successful results. Such experimentation also occurred in Chopin's smaller Warsaw-period genres, which demonstrate his growing ability to transcend the relatively static, symmetrical tonal plans characteristic of the earliest mazurkas and polonaises by means of 'dynamic', goal-directed progressions that achieve greater structural momentum[28] – a technique even more firmly established when he wrote the concertos.

Another such technique was that of 'ornamental melody', apparent above all in the hauntingly beautiful Nocturne in E minor (posthumously published as Op. 72 No. 1), in which embellishment serves as the melodic essence, not mere surface decoration. Developed in Chopin's highly ornate polonaises from earlier in the period, this art of embellishment would influence the thematic material in the first and second movements of both concertos. The third movements, by contrast, reflect a technique principally fostered in the mazurkas, which, like their folk models, thrive upon the obsessive repetition of tiny cells – motives, melodic fragments, grace notes and other ornaments. By repeating ideas throughout the seemingly disparate parts of a work, Chopin ensured an 'organic' unity for his mazurkas – and indeed the concertos – which the eclectic virtuoso music from the 1820s could never possess.

In summary, then, the cumulative weight of Chopin's previous music helped him attain a new level of artistry in the two concertos. Here the *stile brillante* was 'brought to perfection',[29] his ornamental melody refined as never before, a sensitivity to momentum and shape realised, and a more profound synthesis of detail and whole effected. The concertos distil all the influences from Chopin's formative years into a unique stylistic voice, one to be articulated in a wide range of music throughout the following two decades. Even the twenty-year-old composer-pianist recognised his achievement in these strikingly mature works.

Creation

Genesis

After his Vienna triumph in August 1829, Chopin returned to Warsaw newly committed to a virtuoso career, and before long he embarked on his first concerto with that goal in mind. His earliest mention of the F minor Concerto appears in a letter to his friend Tytus Woyciechowski dated 3 October 1829, confessing that his 'ideal' – Konstancja Gładkowska, a young singer he had long admired – had inspired the slow movement. On 20 October, he told Tytus: 'Elsner has praised the Adagio of my concerto. He says it is original; but I don't wish to hear any opinions on the Rondo just yet as I am not quite satisfied with it.'[1] In mid November Chopin commented that the third movement was still incomplete, and several months passed before the concerto's first public airing on 17 March 1830 at the Teatr Narodowy, conducted by Kurpiński. This concert – Chopin's Warsaw debut – had such success (despite his own misgivings) that it was repeated on the 22nd with a larger, more resonant piano.

By then the E minor Concerto was underway. Chopin reported to Tytus on 27 March 1830 that 'I shall be finishing the first Allegro of my second concerto before the holidays',[2] and on 15 May that although the Rondo was unfinished, the first movement was done, as was the second movement, of which he observed:

> It is not meant to create a powerful effect; it is rather a Romance, calm and melancholy, giving the impression of someone looking gently towards a spot which calls to mind a thousand happy memories. It is a kind of reverie in the moonlight on a beautiful spring evening. Hence the accompaniment is muted: that is, the violins are muffled by a sort of comb which fits over the strings and gives them a nasal and silvery tone . . .[3]

Chopin had finished the concerto by the end of August 1830, inform-ing Tytus on the 31st of upcoming rehearsals and mentioning that his friend Józef Linowski was copying the orchestral parts (perhaps to avoid the confusion that had occurred in Vienna due to his own illegible parts for the *Rondo à la krakowiak*). After several rehearsals, he declared on 22 September: 'My second concerto . . . is far too original and I shall end up by not being able to learn it myself . . . The Rondo is effective and the first movement Allegro is impressive.'[4] Those sentiments were echoed by distinguished musicians in attendance at the rehearsals and the public debut on 11 October 1830, although, as we shall see, the press response was more subdued than in the case of the F minor seven months earlier.

Both the consistency of Chopin's models and the remarkable speed with which the two concertos were written explain the parallels between them. Each has three movements: the first ('Maestoso' in the F minor, 'Allegro maestoso' in the E minor) follows the conventional alternation of tutti and solo sections described in Chapter 1, although within the solo sections the 'passagework' surrounding the themes is not virtuosic but expressive in function. The slow movements resemble Chopin's nocturnes in their melodic and accompanimental figuration: the Larghetto from the F minor is in a ternary form, with an arresting recita-tive section at its heart, while the Romance (also 'Larghetto') from the E minor Concerto has a more complex formal scheme featuring three statements of the main theme interspersed by other material. Both third movements draw upon Polish dance idioms – the F minor's Allegro vivace contains mazurka-like themes, while the E minor's Rondo derives from the krakowiak – and both alternate between thematic and episodic sections, with a brilliant 'finale' at the end. Of course, many differences between the two concertos could also be cited; the analysis in Chapter 4 identifies these, along with important deviations from Chopin's models.[5]

Little insight into the compositional process can be gained from the surviving source material, which is almost nonexistent in the case of the E minor and only somewhat more abundant for the F minor. The earliest source is a fragment from the latter's first movement – bars 225–6, jotted on the same sheet as a sketch of the Trio Op. 8 – and there is a second-piano arrangement of the orchestral accompaniment from the second and third movements hastily prepared by Chopin's friend and amanuensis Julian Fontana (probably for his own use: the first published version for two pianos did not appear until 1860).[6] But the most interesting, if problematic, document is a partial autograph from the mid 1830s containing the orchestral parts in an unknown hand, with the solo part (including orchestral tuttis reduced for piano) added later by Chopin. It is possible that the score served as an engraver's manuscript (*Stichvorlage*) for the German first edition, published by Breitkopf & Härtel in 1836 – but even that is uncertain.[7] The only known autograph source for the E minor is the *Stichvorlage* of the first orchestral tutti reduced for piano, prepared by Chopin for the solo-piano version published by Maurice Schlesinger in 1833; this deviates slightly from the orchestral accompaniment itself. For the second and third movements, Auguste Franchomme's second-piano reduction of the orchestra part survives, possibly, like Fontana's of the F minor, intended for use in teaching or (less likely) public performance.[8] Chopin himself appears never to have played the concertos accompanied by a second piano, instead performing them as solos, with chamber ensemble or, as in his Warsaw debuts, with full orchestra.

First performances, first reviews, first editions

Concerts

Chopin's legendary reputation as a pianist arose from fewer than two dozen public performances throughout his career, and of these roughly half featured one of the two concertos – particularly the E minor, which served as something of a warhorse for the budding composer-pianist. After the Warsaw debuts of the F minor on 17 and 22 March 1830 and the E minor on 11 October 1830, Chopin played the E minor Concerto in various European cities: first, Breslau, in an impromptu concert in the Merchants' Hall on 8 November 1830, which featured the Rondo, possibly also the Romance, with orchestral accompaniment; next, Vienna, where he performed the entire concerto with orchestra in a benefit concert at the Kärntnerthortheater on 11 June 1831;[9] then, Munich, in the hall of the Philharmonic Society on 28 August 1831 (possibly with orchestra);[10] and finally, Paris, where, over four years, he performed one or more movements on at least five occasions, either as a solo or, more likely, accompanied by orchestra or string ensemble. There was also a performance of the entire E minor Concerto on 12 March 1838 in Rouen, probably with chamber accompaniment.[11] But it was the five Paris concerts that both secured Chopin's reputation and eventually persuaded him to abandon altogether his aspirations as a composer-pianist.

His Paris debut took place before a glittering audience at the Salons de Pleyel on 26 February 1832, and he chose to perform the E minor Concerto (not the F minor, as frequently claimed), most likely accompanied by string quintet. Jean-Jacques Eigeldinger writes:

> The consequences of this first concert for Chopin's career in Paris proved of the utmost importance: with the weight of his authority, [François-Joseph] Fétis underscored in the musical press the composer's originality and his qualities as a performer; the editors [Aristide] Farrenc and Maurice Schlesinger . . . rushed to offer to engrave the works in his portfolio; the piano maker Camille Pleyel definitively attached himself to the artist . . .

Furthermore, 'the first-rank salons of the capital opened their doors to him', his reputation as a teacher began to develop and other composers started to use themes from his works in paraphrases.[12] Repeated airings of the E minor soon followed: on 20 May 1832, at a concert sponsored by the Prince de la Moskowa at the Salle du Conservatoire, where Chopin played the first movement with orchestra for the first time in Paris, under the conductor Narcisse Girard;[13] on 25 April 1833, at the Athénée musical, Hôtel-de-Ville, which featured an 'ADAGIO et Rondo d'un concerto pour Piano, composé et exécuté par M. CHOPIN, de Varsovie',[14] probably with orchestra, again under Girard; on 14 December 1834 (not the 7th, as originally advertised), at Berlioz's third benefit concert for Harriet Smithson, in the Salle du Conservatoire, where the Romance was played with orchestra, yet again conducted by Girard; and finally, on 5 April 1835, in a concert at the Théâtre-Italien to benefit Polish refugees, which Chopin himself sponsored, performing the entire E minor Concerto with orchestra, under François-Antoine Habeneck. This last appearance – the sole occasion in his Paris career when he played the complete concerto with orchestra – was a decisive turning point, for although the principal review speaks of success (not without bias, however: it was in a journal owned by Chopin's publisher), Chopin himself was bitterly disappointed at the reception to both his playing and the piece itself – a work on which he had pinned his hopes as a composer-pianist, not once, it seems, having played the F minor Concerto or his other works with orchestra before the Paris public.[15] After performing the *Grande polonaise* in Habeneck's own concert three weeks later (26 April 1835) at the Salle du Conservatoire (Société des Concerts), he appeared in public on very few occasions thereafter, and never again with orchestra.

Reception

Reviews exist of virtually all these performances (see Appendix 1, p. 101), and Chopin's correspondence also reveals early reactions to the concertos as he played them. For instance, on 27 March 1830, shortly after the F minor's Warsaw premiere, he wrote to Tytus:

> my first concert . . . did not make on the general public the impression I thought it would. The first Allegro of my concerto, which relatively few could grasp, called forth applause, but it seems to me that people felt they had to show interest ('Ah, something new!') and pretend to be connoisseurs. The Adagio and Rondo produced the greatest effect and exclamations of sincere admiration could be heard.[16]

The *Powszechny dziennik krajowy* of 19 March 1830 published a particularly fulsome review:

> Harmony is at the very heart of M. Chopin's concerto. It permeates each solo from beginning to end. The melodies . . . so lovely and pleasing in themselves . . . [are] grounded on this well-proportioned harmonic foundation. The typical excesses peculiar to new composers are nowhere to be seen. Each tutti is perfectly structured to blend imperceptibly with the solo passages in such a way that the delighted listener can scarcely distinguish the one from the other . . . The performance was entirely in keeping with the spirit of the composition. Never did the pianist try to exploit the technical difficulties, the bravura passages, or the tender, lyrical melodies in order to shine at the expense of the overall musical effect . . . His playing seemed to say to the listener: 'This is not me; this is music!'[17]

The *Kurier warszawski* of 18 March 1830 observed: 'The Adagio of this concerto drew the attention of the connoisseurs for its excellence not only in the way it was performed but also in the way it was conceived',[18] while the *Kurier polski* wrote on 20 March: '[Chopin's] compositions are particularly characterized by the way he incorporates his lovely and original melodies and bold, brilliant passages . . . into a unified whole. The listener is struck by the combination of his beautiful gift for composition with his playing, which displays such a depth of feeling and a dexterity that can overcome the greatest difficulties as if they didn't exist at all.'[19] Two days after the repeat performance on 22 March, the *Kurier polski* remarked that 'all his compositions sound like improvisations because he doesn't try to imitate others but always brings forth something new, fresh – in a word, inspired', and on 26 March that his playing 'seems to be the natural result of his compositions'; also, that 'the beauty of each work was related to the orchestral accompaniment, which never distorted or overpowered the principal instrument. On the contrary, the accompaniment served to augment and ennoble its beauty.'[20]

As for the E minor Concerto, a review in the *Powszechny dziennik krajowy* published two days after the rehearsal on 22 September 1830 called it '*a work of genius*' and praised its 'originality and graceful conception', 'abundance of imaginative ideas', 'perfect orchestration' and 'masterful execution',[21] while Chopin himself wrote to Tytus on 18 September after an earlier rehearsal that the Rondo was considered 'most attractive (that's because it is easiest to understand)', and on 5 October that 'Kurpiński spoke at length of its originality and Elsner of its rhythm'.[22] The press was virtually silent after the premiere on 11 October (possibly because of tighter censorship in response to rising political tensions): the only known review, published the next day in the *Kurier warszawski*, merely describes it as 'one of the most sublime of all musical works'[23] – warm enough praise, but hardly the ecstatic tribute paid to the F minor earlier that year. Chopin reported to Tytus on 12 October: 'I have never before managed to play so well with orchestra. The audience enjoyed my piano–playing'.[24]

After performing the Rondo and, possibly, the Romance of the E minor in Breslau about a fortnight later, Chopin wrote to his family on 9 November that the Germans had declared: '"How light his touch is!" . . . – but about the composition itself, not a word . . . One . . . local expert

. . . praised the novelty of the *form*, saying he had never yet heard anything quite like it . . . Perhaps he understood better than any of them'.[25] A Viennese critic chided him in the *Allgemeine Theaterzeitung* of 18 June 1831 for being 'a little too free with his tempi' in his performance of the E minor a week earlier,[26] while, according to *Flora* (30 August 1831), his Munich appearance revealed 'an outstanding virtuosity':

> A lovely delicacy along with a beautiful and individualistic interpretation of the themes was characteristic of his cultivated style. On the whole the work was brilliant and well written but without any particular originality or depth except for the main theme and middle section of the Rondo, which display a unique charm in their peculiar combination of melancholy and light-hearted passages.[27]

Chopin shed further light on the Germans' reactions in a letter to Tytus dated 12 December 1831, stating that 'the Rhinelanders – the Lindpaintners, Bergs, Stuntzes, Schunkes – and all Bavaria could not praise highly enough' his E minor Concerto.[28]

Fétis' account of Chopin's Paris debut on 26 February (*Revue musicale*, 3 March 1832) is especially incisive:

> M. Chopin performed a concerto that caused as much astonishment as pleasure because of the novelty of its melodic ideas as well as its figurations, modulations and form in general. His melodies are soulful, his keyboard writing imaginative; originality prevails throughout. But mixed in with the qualities I have just identified are such weaknesses as over-rich modulations and a disordered succession of phrases, so that sometimes one had the impression of listening to an improvisation rather than composed music . . . As a performer the young artist also deserves praise. His playing is elegant, effortless and graceful, and possesses brilliance and clarity.[29]

Six days after the concert on 20 May 1832, Fétis noted in the *Revue musicale* that the concerto – a 'brilliant success' in its Paris premiere – 'was less well received on this occasion, which can be attributed, without doubt, to the rather heavy orchestration and the weak sound that Chopin extracts from the piano', whereas at Berlioz's concert on 14 December 1834, the slow movement was 'ravishing' (according to *Le Pianiste* on the 20th),[30] having, in Berlioz's words,

> plunged the listeners into a sort of calm and ecstatic joy, to which they were not at all accustomed . . . When the last note fell like a pearl into a

golden vase, the audience, absorbed in contemplation, still listening, waited a few moments before clapping. It was like watching the half-tints of an evening twilight dissolve harmoniously, and then remaining motionless in the dark, the eye still fixed on the point of the horizon where the light had just vanished.[31]

The final Paris performance of the E minor Concerto was reviewed by 'R. F.' in the *Gazette musicale* of 12 April 1835:

Chopin's piano concerto, so original, colourful in style, full of ingenious details and fresh themes, was . . . a very great success. It is certainly difficult to avoid monotony in a piano concerto, and music lovers had M. Chopin to thank for the pleasure he gave them, while the professionals admired the talent necessary to succeed in rejuvenating such an old form.[32]

Ernest Legouvé's account of the Rouen concert (*Revue et Gazette musicale de Paris*, 25 March 1838) offers rather more extravagant praise: 'his success was immense! immense! These ravishing melodies, these indescribable delicacies of execution, these melancholy and passionate inspirations, this poetry of performance and composition which captures your mind and your heart – all these penetrated, moved and intoxicated the 500 listeners'.[33]

Publication

By then both concertos had been published, initially the E minor, as Op. 11, in 1833, followed three years later by the F minor, as Op. 21. Each appeared in multiple first editions, issued in Paris, Leipzig and London, in order to ensure maximum copyright protection.[34] The French first edition of Op. 11 was produced by Schlesinger in June 1833 (plate no. 1409), after preliminary negotiations with Farrenc. Dedicated to Kalkbrenner (probably an obligatory act of homage), the work could be bought for 12 francs in solo–piano format, with the orchestral tuttis reduced for piano as noted above; for 24 francs 'avec Orchestre' – that is, with a set of orchestral parts (no full score was published for several decades); or for 18 francs with quintet accompaniment, the five parts of which are identical to those of the orchestral strings, with important wind and brass passages printed in small notes for performance by the quintet. It was only natural that Chopin should first publish the work that had made his name in Paris; even so (Eigeldinger cautions), 'as there is no known complete autograph or contemporary copy, one cannot guarantee that the Concerto in E minor played at Pleyel's and then at the Prince de la Moskowa's concert corresponds note for note to the version engraved by Schlesinger, nor, by extension, whether or not the cut proposed by Kalkbrenner [in November 1831] was carried out'.[35] It is also uncertain what happened to the 'brilliant and impressive cadenza' referred to in Kanne's review from 1831.

What is clear is that Schlesinger's Op. 11 closely corresponds to the German and English first editions, published respectively by Kistner (in September 1833; plate nos. 1020, 1021 and 1022 – i.e. orchestra, quintet and solo formats) and Wessel (date uncertain, possibly May 1834; plate no. 1086), in part because each was engraved from corrected proof sheets of the French first edition.[36] Nevertheless, despite their common source, variants differentiate the three editions – both typographical errors and alternative readings either imposed by house editors or introduced by Chopin himself at some publication stage.[37] Such discrepancies are one reason why the modern editor's task is so vexed in the case of Chopin's music, even Op. 11 with its limited autograph sources; they also impinge on performance, affecting features like pedalling, slurring and the very notes.

Editorial matters are more complicated for Op. 21, published by Breitkopf & Härtel in April 1836 (plate no. 5654), Wessel in May 1836 (plate no. 1642) and Schlesinger between July and September 1836 (plate no. 1940). Although ready for publication several years earlier, and of course composed before the E minor Concerto, the F minor was released at a respectable distance from Chopin's 'warhorse' for commercial reasons (not, as some have claimed, because Chopin had lost the parts en route to Paris or had left the score in Warsaw), just as his 'third concerto', possibly available for publication as early as 1834, was delayed to avoid interference with Op. 11's sales.[38] It is not known what documents served as *Stichvorlagen* for these various editions of Op. 21.[39] Virtually identical layouts and textual commonalities imply that the Wessel edition was prepared from proof sheets provided by Schlesinger (as was the case with Op. 11),[40] although details in the English first edition also suggest the influence of the previously released Breitkopf score. The

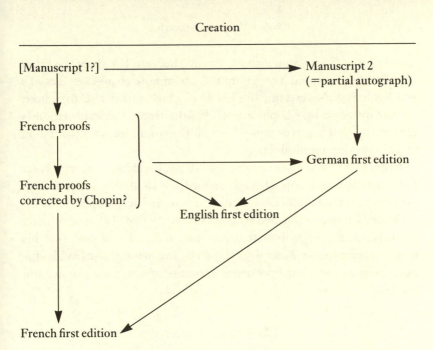

Figure 2.1 F minor Concerto: hypothetical stemma

latter was printed at a time when Chopin's long-established practice of sending corrected proof sheets to Germany for use as *Stichvorlagen* changed to one of furnishing the German publisher with autograph or scribal copies – perhaps the result of discussions during Chopin's visit to Leipzig in Autumn 1835. It might be that the partial autograph referred to earlier – which could have been hand-delivered to Breitkopf by Chopin himself – served as a *Stichvorlage*: it seems to have been written out with this in mind (recall Chopin's instructions to the printer), although the apparent lack of engraver's markings (*Stechereintragungen*) indicates otherwise. Different stemmatic analyses can be posited, but the one in Figure 2.1 seems most likely. According to this scenario, an earlier autograph – probably Chopin's working manuscript from Warsaw – served as the basis of the French first edition, proof sheets of which were then forwarded to Leipzig and London in the normal manner, with *Stechereintragungen* entered on these.[41] The surviving partial autograph then offered Breitkopf a secondary, more authoritative *Stichvorlage*, thus explaining readings in the German first edition absent from the French or English scores (note however that this manuscript was not strictly followed by the German publisher). Finally, because Breitkopf's edition appeared first, it could have prompted last-minute changes in Wessel's and Schlesinger's versions, the latter of which might also have been further modified by Chopin himself.[42] Admittedly this explanation is conjectural, but it solves most if not all the conundrums surrounding Op. 21's mysterious production.

Echoing the cautionary remark cited above, Eigeldinger observes that as there is no manuscript of the F minor from 1830, it is 'impossible to say whether or not the 1835 version [i.e. the partial autograph] conforms to the one Chopin performed six years earlier'.[43] The likelihood of exact correspondence seems remote given the continual evolution that his music experienced in general, as shown by the many glosses in his students' copies and their eyewitness accounts of Chopin's playing and teaching.

Chopin as teacher

Chopin taught his students a number of concertos, including Hummel's in A minor and B minor, Mendelssohn's in G minor, Weber's *Konzert-stück*, and at least some by Field and Beethoven. He also used Op. 11 and Op. 21 as teaching pieces, particularly the first movements. Both concertos were played by Camille Dubois (née O'Meara) and Elise Peruzzi, while Caroline Hartmann and Carl Filtsch studied one or more movements from Op. 11 and Jane Stirling and Friederike Müller one or more from Op. 21. According to first-hand reports, Chopin often accompanied them on 'a cottage piano [*pianino*] by the side of the grand piano on which he gave his lessons', performing the role of the orchestra 'most wonderfully',[44] whether privately or in front of a *matinée* audience.

The glosses in scores used by his pupils and associates, whether in Chopin's own hand or transcribed by the latter, reveal much about his playing and teaching styles. Some correct typographical errors or omissions: for instance, in Franchomme's copy of Op. 21 '*pp*' was reinstated in bar 1 of the Larghetto, while in Stirling's Op. 11 flats were added before the left-hand Es in bar 658 of the first movement. Others reflect Chopin's ongoing creative involvement with the music, such as the improvisatory variants in bars 153 and 583 of the Allegro maestoso from

Op. 11 and bars 58, 59 and 61 of the Romance.[45] Stirling's score of Op. 11
and Dubois' of both concertos (all in solo-piano format) are filled with
glosses, many in pencil (some Chopin's), others in ink (entered by the
student, often over a pencilled original).[46] Fingerings and accidentals
are most abundant, but one-off emendations include the left-hand
accompaniment (arpeggios, then chords) notated in the Larghetto's
recitative section in Stirling's copy of Op. 21, destined for use in solo performance, or Chopin's pencilled 'Adagio' on the title page of her Op. 11 –
which happens to be the movement with the greatest number of glosses.
In Dubois' Op. 21 (the first movement of which contains most of
Chopin's indications) we find dynamics, articulation markings, phrasing
and – of particular interest – liaisons between the hands, as in bars 7, 9,
26 and 75 of the Larghetto, where the first note of a right-hand arpeg-
giated ornament is to be played on the beat with the left hand, in keeping
with eighteenth- rather than nineteenth-century performance practice.
Such liaisons also appear in her Op. 11 score, for instance in bars 255 and
(problematically, given the huge leap that follows!) 403 of the Allegro
maestoso, the former analogous to the *cercar della nota*, one of many
ornaments deriving from the *bel canto* style that so inspired Chopin.[47]

Other evidence in the concertos of an eighteenth-century performance legacy can be seen in the many *fioriture* and *gruppetti* (which,
according to Jan Kleczyński, 'should be played more slowly at the
commencement and accelerated towards the end');[48] 'embellishments,
minute or luxuriant, whose performance requires both a mastery of the
keyboard and the evanescence of spontaneous creativity';[49] ascending
chromatic glissandos (*portamento*) and their inversions (*strascino*); *par-
lando* effects; trills beginning on the upper or lower auxiliary note,
usually played simultaneously with the bass; 'long appoggiaturas';
fingerings; and, of course, rubato, which in various passages also reflects
the influence of Polish folk music.[50]

Particular insight into Chopin's performance aesthetic and his
conception of the E minor Concerto can be gained from Wilhelm von
Lenz's first-hand description of a remarkable dress rehearsal on two
pianos organised by Chopin for his talented pupil Filtsch, who performed at least the first movement of Op. 11 on various occasions (for
instance, at Baron de Rothschild's salon on 11 January 1843):[51]

In this piece the pianist must be first tenor, first soprano – always a singer and a bravura singer in the runs, which Chopin wanted the pianist to take pains to render in the *cantabile* style. This was the way he taught Filtsch . . . to understand this first movement. At that time (1842), Chopin himself no longer played the piece, as he had already given up performing in public. Still, he played us the themes indescribably beautifully and gave us hints for playing the runs and passage-work. He wanted the runs *cantabile*, with a certain measure of strength and bravura within, trying to bring out as much as possible the slightest thematic fragments, using the most delicate touch, even where the runs are no more than runs – which in this piece is the exception. The second and third movements were never mentioned . . . Filtsch studied the work with Chopin solo section by solo section; he was never allowed to play the movement right through, since it would affect Chopin too powerfully; Chopin maintained besides that the entire work's power was contained within each solo section . . .

When at last Filtsch was allowed to play the whole movement – an occasion for which he had prepared himself by Roman Catholic fasting and prayer as well as by reading the score under Chopin's direction (practising had been forbidden) – Chopin said, 'Now this movement is sufficiently "in place" for us to play it: I'll be your orchestra' . . . With his incomparable way of accompanying, Chopin evoked all the ingenious and elusive qualities of the orchestration. He played from memory. I have never heard anything comparable to that first tutti as he played it himself at the piano. As for the lad, he worked marvels. It was the experience of a lifetime.[52]

Chopin's special attachment to the E minor Concerto by no means suggests indifference to the F minor: on the contrary, Carl Mikuli reports that Op. 21 'was particularly dear to Chopin's heart', while Liszt refers to his 'marked predilection' for the second movement, 'which he liked to play frequently'.[53] It is certain, therefore, that Chopin would have been troubled and perplexed by the interpretative responses to both concertos after they left his hands to make their own way through the world. Only rarely would they again inspire a reaction like Lenz's: once divorced from the unique performance aesthetic that had guided their creation, the concertos no longer communicated the expressive message that Chopin himself had brought to life as composer, performer and teacher.

3

Interpretation

On interpreting Chopin

Musical meaning is elusive and ephemeral – like music itself. The identity of a musical work continually evolves as it experiences successive interpretations,[1] and the degree to which it can endure a multiplicity of readings without suffering 'depletion' may be one measure of its aesthetic value. In this sense Chopin's concertos are truly great works, for they have weathered a vast range of response yet still invite new and different interpretations, their musical content too rich in potential for individual readings to exhaust.[2]

Chopin reception over the past 150 years is characterised in general by extraordinary diversity – in part because of the relative nonspecificity of his music's expressive language (as opposed, say, to the more programmatic idiom of composers like Liszt).[3] It is nevertheless possible to trace patterns within the welter of critical reaction to the composer's music, one of these a progression from the highly personalised responses common in the mid to late nineteenth century, through the ostensibly more rigorous structuralist critiques of this century, to the 'reconciliatory' synthesis of the subjective and the objective typical of recent scholarship.[4] This dialectical framework – like Samson's model of Chopin reception as a 'dispersal of meanings' in the nineteenth century followed by a 'closure of meaning' in the twentieth[5] – takes as its starting point the nineteenth-century listener's tendency to poeticise, to programmatise, to translate a musical work into a narrative, whether historical or biographical. Thus arose a class of writing about music using metaphor or analogy as its 'principal tool',[6] and attempting to capture in prose the sense and experience of music as sound. More standardised perceptual tools emerged towards the end of the nineteenth century as a result of the formalist aesthetic championed by Eduard Hanslick and later implemented by the likes of Heinrich Schenker and Hugo Leichtentritt, whose diverse analytical approaches shared an emphasis on the music's inner construction rather than its putative expressive message – on music defined 'in its own terms', on structure, on architecture. Schenker himself was of course acutely sensitive to music's temporal progression, scorning those who analysed 'by eye', not 'ear', but, ironically, the school of thought he so disdained has dominated much twentieth-century analysis, placing a premium on synchronic structural integrity at the expense of the diachronically unfolding flow of events that characterises music in sound. This occurred with particularly invidious results in the case of Chopin's concertos, which, conceived with the medium of performance at heart, unduly suffered as 'performance and text were prised apart' in a 'drama of separation'[7] enacted in critical writing, editing and performance.

Recent trends have seen the greater fusion of synchronic and diachronic modes of understanding and of subjective and objective response in the dialectical synthesis previously referred to. Such a fusion will also be undertaken in Chapter 4, in an attempt to re-evaluate this music in terms compatible with the spirit that guided its conception, and thus to shed new light on its potential meaning and significance. Before this, however, it will be instructive to trace the tortuous journey charted by the two works through the worlds of criticism, editing and performance during the past century and a half.

Critics

Several leitmotifs permeate the early reviews cited in Chapter 2, all of which respond to the concertos as performed by Chopin. Perhaps the most prevalent concerns their originality – their 'abundance of imaginative ideas', 'novelty of form', unconventional figuration, 'freshness', 'genius'. Although criticised for 'over-rich' harmonies and a certain 'disorder', and despite his 'weak sound' and the 'rather heavy orchestration', the concertos under Chopin's hands possessed grace, elegance and beauty. Their effect was that of an improvisation, his playing at one with the music in emphasising expression, not mere virtuosity.

The literature on the two concertos as published echoes some of these themes, but from about 1850 onwards they inspired new, often less favourable opinions. The earliest writing on Op. 11 focuses on the virtuoso element. Ludwig Rellstab considers its difficulties unprecedented and unjustified, arising from 'an extremely uncomfortable lie of the figuration within the hand',[8] while Gottfried Fink finds it 'enormously hard' to play 'purely, securely, powerfully, delicately' and with freedom of movement. Noting that listeners would respond differently from the pianist ('what more do the hands need?'), he implies that the concerto – which 'exudes a unique spirit' – is better to play than to hear.[9] Two English critics are exceptionally scathing: J. W. Davison discerns 'the most palpable errors and ugliness' and calls Chopin an 'expert doer of little things . . . [which] are sullied by extravagant affectation, and a straining after originality',[10] while the *Musical Magazine* brands Op. 11 a 'heterogeneous mass', a '*compound of filthy sounds*' consisting of 'the most ludicrous and extravagant passages – modulations we cannot call them, for they "*Out Herod*" every thing of the kind we ever before heard . . . It is altogether beneath criticism; and we shall be much surprised, if even John Bull's silly predilection for foreign trash will induce him to purchase such a farrago of nonsense and *caterwauling*.'[11]

In his diachronic analysis of the Maestoso from Op. 21 (which he considers more intelligible than Op. 11, and thus more likely to make a 'general impression'), Fink assesses such elements as the first theme (to be played flexibly, not in strict time), the second theme (whose 'darker nuances' derive from the embellishment) and the figuration (which has a unifying effect, 'so that the whole is not difficult for the listener to comprehend'), as well as the orchestral accompaniment.[12] François Stoepel's account of Op. 11 is similar in format, underscoring the music's emotional logic and large-scale plan, namely, a progression from the first movement's tumultuous despair through the Romance's serenity to the light-hearted, lively Rondo. His detailed breakdown highlights Chopin's ability 'to ally the rich harmony to an original melody and to share between the two hands an often difficult task instead of tiring only one by long and precipitous figuration'; nevertheless, the virtuoso passages 'are all the more difficult in execution because they bear no resemblance whatsoever to those ordinarily encountered in the works of other composers'.[13] Equally reflective of the music's process is Schumann's description of the two concertos as a phenomenon best approached 'through the senses', impossible to grasp 'from all angles in its full height and depth'.[14]

Later reactions such as Liszt's, Louis Ehlert's and (to some extent) Lenz's anticipate the formalist critiques that would become normative after Frederick Niecks's influential biography of the composer, which set in stone the main themes of virtually all subsequent writing on the concertos. According to Liszt, Chopin imprisoned his thought and violated his genius in writing the concertos, which possess 'more *volonté* than inspiration'; even so, 'these essays shine by a rare distinction of style, containing passages of great interest and fragments of a surprising grandeur'. In particular, the Larghetto from Op. 21 is 'of an ideal perfection'.[15] Ehlert echoes Liszt's view that Chopin's originality and freedom of conception inhibited his concerto technique: he could not master large forms and lacked contrapuntal and orchestration skills.[16] As for Lenz, the contrast between his enthusiasm for Op. 11's Allegro maestoso (the sole movement he witnessed under Chopin's hands) and his dismissal of the Romance and Rondo and Op. 21 as a whole could hardly be starker. 'Only the first movement [of Op. 11] is a convincing masterpiece; the Larghetto is a tiresome Nocturne, the Rondo a Hummel. One regrets that the great pianists do not more often play the first movement as a completely independent concerto.' Op. 21 lacks ideas and is conventional – 'without interest in its invention, the entire outline itself immature and fragmentary', the passagework derivative. 'The cantabile style of the Larghetto is in an empty, shallow Hummelesque vein', and although the last movement has some merit, its main idea bears little fruit: 'from a theme of this sort one cannot construct a finale'. Moreover, 'the orchestral part, which in the E minor Concerto was so interesting, is relegated to a secondary role in [Op. 21]; the structure of the movements is superficial and meaningless'.[17]

Niecks's commentary[18] significantly differs from Lenz's only in lavishing praise on Op. 21 while savaging Op. 11, but its impact on the reception of Chopin's concertos was without equal. In his view, Chopin 'lacked the peculiar qualities, natural and acquired, requisite for a successful cultivation of the larger forms': 'his arguments are poor and the conclusions often wanting', devoid of 'a sustained and dominating intellectual power'. Furthermore, he had no aptitude for orchestral writing, 'and the nature of his material accorded little with the size of the

structure and the orchestral frame . . . Are not these confessions of intimate experiences, these moonlight sentimentalities, these listless
dreams, etc., out of place in the gaslight glare of concert-rooms . . . ?' In
writing for other instruments, 'Chopin's originality is gone': 'every new
entry of the orchestra precipitates you from the delectable regions of
imagination to the joyless deserts of the actual'. But 'such is the charm,
loveliness, delicacy, elegance, and brilliancy of the details, that one again
and again forgives and forgets their shortcomings as wholes'.

For Niecks, the first movement of Op. 21 is salvaged by Chopin's 'tale
full of sweet melancholy in a strain of lovely, tenderly-intertwined
melody', and the third movement by 'its feminine softness and rounded
contours, its graceful, gyrating, dance-like motions, its sprightliness and
frolicsomeness . . . Unless I quote every part and particle, I feel I cannot
do justice to it. The exquisite ease and grace, the subtle spirit . . . defy
description'. The listener gets so carried away that 'no time is left him to
reflect and make objection with reference to the whole'. As for Op. 11,
the first movement's 'elongated form . . . compares disadvantageously
with the greater compactness' of Op. 21, 'and makes still more sensible
the monotony resulting from the key-relation of the constituent parts,
the tonic being the same in both subjects . . . [and] not relieved till the
commencement of the working-out section. The re-entrance of the
second subject brings, at last, something of a contrast.' In short, 'those
powerful levers, key-relation and contrast', were not understood by
Chopin.[19] 'Still, the movement is certainly not without beauty, although
the themes appear somewhat bloodless, and the passages are less brilliant
and piquant than those in the F minor Concerto. Exquisite softness and
tenderness distinguish the melodious parts, and Chopin's peculiar
coaxing tone is heard in the semiquaver passage marked *tranquillo* of the
first subject.' In contrast, the Romance exudes a 'cloying sweetness'
while the coquettish third movement yields 'tricksy surprises'. He concludes: 'What a pity that Chopin should have set so many beautiful
thoughts and fancies in such a frame and thereby marred them!'

Niecks – author of the first scholarly monograph on Chopin – directly
or indirectly influenced such authors as James Huneker,[20] Leichtentritt,[21] Adolf Weissmann,[22] Bernard Scharlitt,[23] Gerald Abraham,[24]
Arthur Hedley,[25] Herbert Weinstock[26] and Michael Roeder[27] in their
assessments of the concertos, thus prompting a coalescence of critical

response into three recurrent, almost inevitable criticisms. These concern Chopin's *poor control of form and tonal structure*; the music's *lack of development and organic unity*; and the *inept orchestration*. Furthermore, like Niecks, most of these authors grudgingly acknowledge that beauty of detail is the music's saving grace, especially the effusive ornamentation, which compensates for the formal weaknesses, hack orchestration and eclectic musical material. Such thoughts colour the writing of even the most astute commentators.[28]

Of course other themes have emerged in the literature on the concertos published after Niecks – for instance, regarding their technical demands[29] and emotional content.[30] The two works have even been described as paradigms of the 'brilliant romantic piano concerto' – by Schering and Engel among others[31] – in a reversal of the ubiquitous early recognition of their originality. But perhaps most striking are certain attempts to encapsulate the concertos in terms of *performance* – as 'live' phenomena to be experienced in time.

One example is Johannes Merkel's *Klaviermusikführer* on Op. 11 (published in 1898), which perspicaciously notes that Chopin's concertos were 'held in high regard by piano virtuosos' but not critics. Nevertheless, 'even the harshest critic has to acknowledge the fact that both works, when performed in the spirit of their creator, have an unusually profound effect on every part of our concertgoing public'.[32] His blow-by-blow descriptive analysis is akin to Hermann Kretschmar's, whose 1902 monograph refrains from synchronic assessments like Niecks's. As a Pole, he says, Chopin may have poorly grasped German *Sonatenkunst*, but often he achieves a correct relationship between keyboard and orchestral accompaniment, which is not a stopgap. And Chopin was by no means unable to handle large forms: instead, his formal understanding was innovative. In Op. 11's first movement, the flouting of standard sonata rules unites the themes (as opposed to the usual opposition), whereas in the development, expression, not bravura showmanship, is the goal: 'The virtuosity . . . serves a poetic idea.'[33]

Between the formalist attacks instigated by Niecks in 1888 and levelled on the concertos throughout this century, and the 'experiential' responses of Lenz, Merkel, Kretschmar and others, lurks a dichotomy pertinent to all style-criticism and analysis – namely, between a synoptic, synchronic, work-oriented approach shaped by the formalist aesthetic, and a dynamic, diachronic, listener-oriented experiencing of music, the latter having gradually been eclipsed by the former in scholarly writing after 1900 or so (as stated above). This virtual eradication has had grim consequences for Chopin's concertos, causing them to be viewed on a slab, inert and inanimate, rather than in 'living sound'. It is high time to revitalise them, explicitly recognising Chopin's compositional goals and performance ethos and the 'central assumption' of the brilliant style – that 'work and performance are inseparably fused',[34] not mutually independent. This will be our task in Chapter 4.

Editors

Musical scores, like dramatic scripts, bear only a partial relation to the performances they inspire. Notoriously unable to capture music's 'living sound' in its full complexity, scores themselves amount to interpretations – at least those prepared after a work's first inscribing by the composer. In the case of Chopin's concertos, editorial interpretations are highly varied, although the pattern identified earlier – from 'dispersal' to 'closure' – once again prevails, encompassing such publication formats as first-edition reprints, collected editions, 'modern' editions (most with second-piano accompaniment) and orchestral scores, as well as transcriptions and arrangements of both solo and orchestral parts (see Appendix 2, p. 103).

Later versions of first editions

As mentioned earlier, the first editions of many Chopin works experienced their own evolution during his lifetime, whereby textual changes as well as typographical corrections infiltrated later impressions with identical plate numbers. This occurred for instance in Breitkopf's first edition of Op. 21, an 1840 reissue of which corrects some (but not all) printing errors, adds or repositions slurs, and removes dynamic and pedal indications (as in bars 232–3 of the Allegro vivace). Once copyright protection expired ten years after Chopin's death (having passed to his legatees in the meantime), more fundamental changes were made to the first-edition plates. For example, a ca 1860 reissue of Breitkopf's Op. 21 reveals novel concordances with the intriguing partial autograph described in Chapter 2, including an alto $e\flat^1$ under the turn in bar 142 and a trill on c^2 (not $b\flat^1$) in bars 335–6 of the Maestoso; a correctly printed bar 80 in the Larghetto (versus the erroneous earlier impressions); and different left-hand pitches in bars 366 and 368 of the Allegro vivace. More radical interventions occur in the Wessel first editions re-released roughly contemporaneously by Ashdown & Parry (Wessel's successor), which, though bearing the same plate numbers (1086 for Op. 11 and 1642 for Op. 21), contain innumerable differences of articulation, dynamics and pitch – particularly in Op. 11, which amounts to a new edition, as does Kistner's Op. 11 from ca 1858. Although its title page approximates the first edition's (apart from some missing punctuation), the music has been entirely reset, despite which the original plate numbers are retained, printed in smaller type underneath a new number '2340'. Deviations from the 1833 issue include editorial slurs, ties, staccato dots and accidentals (such as inauthentic natural signs before the c^3s in bars 233 and 235 of the Rondo, which plague editions to this day) as well as reconfigured rhythms, pedallings and so on.

Collected editions

The first collected editions of Chopin's works appeared shortly after the copyright watershed, among them Richault's (edited by Tellefsen) and Schonenberger's (edited by Fétis), both published in Paris in 1860, followed within a few years by Stellowsky's, Heugel's, and Gebethner & Wolff's.[35] Most, but not all, of the several dozen collected editions released before World War II contain the concertos. Of these, noteworthy examples include Karl Klindworth's (1873–6), Mikuli's (1879), Herrmann Scholtz's (1879), Theodor Kullak's (ca 1880–5), Debussy's (1915–16) and Edouard Ganche's (1932). Each presents an idiosyncratic version of the concertos variably faithful to the first editions.

Klindworth's modestly calls itself the 'seule édition authentique', but it is nothing of the kind, wilfully adding or altering dynamics, fingering, expression markings and slurs. More insidious are textual 'improvements' to Chopin's harmony or voice-leading; for instance, on the last quaver of bar 128 in Op. 21's Maestoso, Klindworth harmonises the right-hand $e\natural^2$ by inserting a (tied) middle C underneath, thus transmuting a chromatic passing note over a dominant (E$\flat$ major) harmony into a contextually garish third-inversion C^7 chord.[36] Eighteen bars later his supplementary quaver rest breaks up Chopin's integral left-hand gesture, while his reconfigured trills at the end of the exposition (adopted by the Paderewski edition, among others) lack the natural logic of the original hand positions.

Mikuli's edition is altogether better, generally remaining close to the first editions (even placing a pedal sign *above* the treble staff in Op. 21, Maestoso, bar 96, as in the earliest impressions). Nevertheless, he adds or repositions phrase markings, pedallings etc., though many fewer than in Klindworth's or, especially, Scholtz's editions. The latter, issued by Peters in various guises (most recently as the work of Bronisław von Poźniak, whose ca 1950 print is typographically almost identical to Scholtz's), moulds the notation according to the editor's performance strategy. For instance, Scholtz splits technically difficult passages between the hands with *m.g.* and *m.d.* indications (Op. 11, Allegro maestoso, bars 661–2) and parses *fioriture* into more 'convenient' but rigid rhythmic groupings (Op. 11, Allegro maestoso, bar 177; Op. 21, Maestoso, bar 145) which destroy the rhythmic flexibility at the heart of Chopin's *bel canto*-influenced keyboard style. Another 'facilitation' occurs in the Romance, where he alters the key signature in bars 80–100 to four flats, enharmonically transposing the prevailing G♯ major to A♭ major.[37] Similar 'refurbishment' occurs in Kullak's edition, which overflows with suggestions to the pianist – both within the music (e.g. 'un poco marcato il basso', in Op. 11, Allegro maestoso, bars 163–4) and in extended footnotes like the following: 'in addition to the sign $<\ >$ added in the base [*sic*] by the editor, a somewhat quicker tempo might also correspond to the more passionate character of the C♯ minor subject' (Op. 11, Romance, bar 64); and 'the impassioned secondary subject (from A[♭] minor on) must not be conceived too much in the Recitative-style' (Op. 21, Larghetto).

As its title makes clear, the edition of Eduard Mertke (1885) explicitly 'corrects' the French and English first editions on which it is based, whereas Ganche's *Oxford Original Edition of Frédéric Chopin* from 1932 attempts the 'publication of his works exactly as he had written them', 'an absolutely genuine and correct text of these masterpieces', 'a completely faithful and reliable edition' in which 'the few indications of fingering' and 'the variety of shades in the "repeats" . . . are Chopin's own'. Despite these and other claims of fidelity, however, Ganche's enterprise is undermined by an over-exclusive reliance on Jane Stirling's scores as source pool and by some questionable readings – as in Op. 11's first movement, where on the downbeat of bar 654 he alters Chopin's daring left-hand F♭s to F♮s, or bar 16 of the Romance, where he instructs the pianist to roll the right hand's third-beat chord, for which Chopin provides fingering enabling a simultaneous attack. Still, the Oxford edition is preferable to the widely used 'Complete Works' of Ignacy Paderewski, Ludwik Bronarski and Józef Turczyński, published from 1949 to 1961, the concertos appearing in two-piano format in 1958, the full score in 1960. Although intended to be definitive and based on a range of documentary sources, the Paderewski edition lacks scholarly authority and should be avoided by pianists, despite occasionally helpful performance suggestions. Its unreliability stems in part from a permissive conflation of secondary source material: both Op. 11 and Op. 21 borrow liberally from Mikuli, Klindworth, Scholtz, Debussy, Mertke and Emil Sauer – as if 'more common'[38] necessarily meant 'best' readings – while not exploiting important primary sources like Stirling's and Dubois' scores. Furthermore, the editors allow harmonic analyses (based on Bronarski's theories) to influence decisions about pitch content and orthography, which they adjust in cases of 'inconsistency' or 'lack of clarity'. Slurrings are also altered (often destroying the 'natural' declamation sought by the composer in performance), parts redistributed, Chopin's fingerings ignored and so forth. In short, the Paderewski edition distorts the original no less than Scholtz's or Klindworth's, however much it purports to 'establish a text which fully reveals Chopin's thought and corresponds to his intentions'.

As stated in the Preface, the best editions at present are Zimmermann's of Op. 11 and Ekier's of Op. 21 (the former in two-piano format, dating from 1989; the latter available both for solo piano and for two pianos – with minor discrepancies between them – dating respectively from 1980 and 1985). Each styles itself an Urtext even though a single authoritative version of Chopin's music can never be achieved, given the existence of multiple autograph sources, first editions, glosses and other variants.[39] Zimmermann's strategy in Henle's Chopin volumes is generally to treat the German first edition as a principal text, and to incorporate 'deviant' readings deemed better (according to inconsistent criteria). In his Op. 11

edition, some interventions are more objectionable than others, such as the regularisation of slurs in bars 425–45 of the first movement or the tacit addition of the rolled-chord sign in bar 16 of the Romance. Still, it is far better than the Paderewski edition, if inferior to Ekier's Op. 21, which, though eclectic, conforms to carefully articulated editorial principles.[40] But without a critical commentary (which remains unpublished, although notes on execution accompany the two-piano 'playing edition'), one cannot identify the provenance of the variants that Ekier either incorporates into the main text or places next to it or in footnotes, in order to give performers additional options. One could quibble with certain readings (for instance, Ekier adds quaver rests in bars 433 and 437 of the Allegro vivace, perpetuating a false tradition stemming from Scholtz, while in bar 260 he needlessly offers an alternative rhythm when Chopin's makes good sense), but this is the best edition of either concerto currently in print – making its absence from music shops especially frustrating.[41]

Editions with second-piano accompaniment

Ekier's solo-piano version, with tutti reductions printed in small notes as in the first editions (and indeed most of those surveyed above), is exceptional for a modern edition in that a second-piano part is now considered essential by publishers. The earliest editions of Op. 11 with an independent piano reduction of the entire orchestral accompaniment were prepared by Heinrich Enke for Kistner during the 1850s and by Tellefsen for Richault (published in 1860); as for Op. 21, there was August Horn's for Breitkopf & Härtel (issued ca 1860–4), as well as Tellefsen's.[42] Others soon followed, the most intriguing Mikuli's of Op. 11 from 1879 (in the supplement to his collected edition). Whereas his second-piano part for Op. 21 basically follows Chopin's own tutti reductions, the accompaniment to Op. 11 omits melodic lines and contrapuntal textures in various key passages, specifies bars of rests while the soloist is also silent, and introduces odd leaps between registers and other anomalies.

Full scores

Kistner published the first orchestral score for Op. 11 during the mid to late 1860s (plate no. 3050), roughly contemporaneous with Breitkopf &

Härtel's of Op. 21 (plate no. 10721).[43] Copied by hand, the latter arranges the instruments in modern fashion (winds, brass, timpani, piano, strings), unlike the partial autograph, this being only one respect in which the two differ. In fact, few details directly stem from the manuscript: the principal model seems to have been the German first edition's parts, with further reference to the tutti reductions (which, incidentally, are printed in the solo part, as in the original version).

Breitkopf & Härtel's 'First Critical Collected Edition' of 1878–80 – both a reflection and a confirmation of Chopin's establishment within the 'classical' canon[44] – contains the concertos in full score in volumes edited by Brahms. Currently available in a Dover reprint, this edition remains authoritative despite some gaffes – for instance, missing 'con sordino' indications in the lower strings at the start of the Romance, a metronome marking of $\downarrow$ = 69 in Op. 21's final movement (versus the more *vivace* $\downarrow$. = 69 of the manuscript and first editions) and the erroneous inclusion in the solo part of orchestral chords in bars 45–7 of the same movement, which were written in large notes in the manuscript but clearly marked 'tutti'.[45] The latter indicates that Brahms consulted the partial autograph, as does the presence of two f^1s in the second-beat 'appoggiatura' in bar 28 of the Larghetto, versus the single f^1 in the three first editions.

Other full scores include Stefan Askenase's (published by Eulenburg in 1957), the Paderewski edition's (prepared by Kazimierz Sikorski) and Michael Stegemann's of Op. 11 (also Eulenburg, from 1985).[46] The most recent of these is also the most disappointing: marred by inaccurate assumptions about the sources,[47] dubious editorial decisions and typographical errors, it is thoroughly unreliable. Eulenburg's new Op. 21, edited by Neubacher, has yet to appear in print.

Transcriptions and arrangements

To the extent that each score surveyed above is an editor's interpretation of Chopin's concertos, then the many transcriptions and arrangements of both pieces are even more so. These have a lengthy history. According to Chopin's letter to Tytus of 27 March 1830, Antoni Orłowski had written mazurkas and waltzes (published by Brzezina) on themes from the F minor Concerto within days of its Warsaw premiere, while Chopin himself borrowed two of its themes for the posthumously published 'Lento con gran espressione' (known as the Nocturne in C♯ minor) written for his sister Ludwika. Later transcriptions[48] include August Wilhelmj's (ca 1870) for violin and piano of both slow movements, and Peter August Schnecker's 'Softly now the light of day' (1903) for voices and organ, based on Op. 21's Larghetto. Less exotic are Ferdinand Schubert's arrangements for piano four-hands from ca 1841 (intended principally for amateurs, and reviewed in the *Allgemeine musikalische Zeitung* of 6 October and 22 December 1841), likewise those for quintet accompaniment from ca 1875. Although Balakirev's solo arrangement of the Romance is still played, Carl Reinecke's Larghetto, which goes to town in the recitative section with a much-enhanced left hand under a right-hand melody in octaves, has grown obsolete, along with Richard Burmeister's cadenza for the Maestoso of Op. 21 (once regularly performed by Paderewski). But amateurs still have at their disposal Noel Fisher's simplified version of Op. 11's first two movements, which tactfully streamlines or omits difficult passages (not to mention the entire Rondo).

Reorchestrations

Of greater interest are the many reorchestrations dating from the late nineteenth century onwards, which attempt to redress the increasingly widespread dissatisfaction with Chopin's 'inadequate' accompaniments. These include, among others, Carl Tausig's (published ca 1880) and Balakirev's (ca 1910) of Op. 11, and Klindworth's (1878) and André Messager's (n.d.) of Op. 21.[49] Predictably, these richly colour and inflate out of proportion Chopin's orchestration, to which melodies and countermelodies are sometimes added for 'developmental' purposes (recall Niecks's criticisms). In Balakirev's, these new parts demonstrate the intrinsic compatibility of seemingly disparate material. For instance, within the 'finale' to the first movement, in bars 625–9 and 637–44, he inserts an obbligato for strings (cellos answered by violins), then winds (oboes answered by flutes) which derives from the main theme in bars 155ff., a subtle link revealing just how 'organic' the music was in the first place. Similarly, the sustained chords originally played by the strings in bars 356–71 of the Rondo, against which the piano tackles some of the most virtuosic figuration in the movement, are transmogrified into a droll restatement of the second theme's ostinato accompaniment, played now by cor anglais, bassoon and pizzicato cello, followed by fragments of the first and second themes in the violins and flutes. New parts also characterise Klindworth's Op. 21 rescoring, as in bars 81ff. of the Allegro vivace, where the horn doubles the piano's inner melody, accompanied by oboes and *divisi* clarinets (editorially marked 'sehr zart', 'espress.', 'dolciss.' and '*pp*' – all within bar 81!). According to Klindworth, the solo part is preserved 'almost intact' (there are in fact many changes), while the orchestral accompaniment is 'completely reworked'. He also alters the first movement's metronome marking to '♩. = 138. (120.)' and tempo to 'Allegro maestoso'. Nevertheless, many fewer emendations occur than in Tausig's widely disseminated Op. 11, which recomposes substantial passages to the extent that the work is unrecognisable as Chopin's. Some of his variants are still performed today.

Although occasionally these new orchestral touches work, in general they strike the listener as risible distortions of Chopin's own creation. Small wonder that both concertos have suffered at the hands of critics since 1880: gaudily embellished, overladen with 'expressivity', and the pitches 'improved' or 'corrected', the music embodied in many editions is indeed worthy of disdain. Given that misinterpretations in editions inevitably provoke misinterpretations in sound, the same might be true of the concertos as recorded – as we shall investigate in the final section of this chapter.

Performers

Both concertos have remained at the heart of the performance canon throughout this century, played by most concert pianists. It is therefore not surprising that over seventy recordings each of Op. 11 and Op. 21 are available on commercial release, in addition to many out of circulation. Before surveying some of the most important (see Appendix 3, p. 105),[50] it will help to define a critical yardstick and to note the recurrence of the familiar 'dispersal to closure' pattern, manifested in a progression from the interpretative freedom enjoyed by pianists in the earlier part of this century, to a narrowing of acceptable performance practice during the past few decades, partly in response to the authenticity movement's strident insistence upon fidelity to the composer.

In Chopin's case, such notions had their first airing over one hundred years ago: towards the end of the nineteenth century, several former pupils – Lenz, Mikuli and Princess Marcelina Czartoryska – expressed concern at the steady supplanting of what they considered the true Chopin performance style by a 'pseudo-tradition' based on unorthodox agogic distortions ('rubato') and other solecisms affecting dynamics, pedalling, tempo and the notes themselves, all perpetrated in Chopin's name but conflicting with his intentions.[51] By then, Chopin was well established in the performance canon, the concertos among his most frequently played works. But the evolution in performing practice that occurred throughout the century proved inimical to these pieces. Merkel's comment quoted earlier speaks volumes about the gulf between the concertos as conceived and as performed around 1900.

This is not to suggest that there has ever been only one 'correct' way to play the music. Even Chopin, who was exacting in matters of interpretation, tolerated a certain flexibility in performance. To Filtsch he remarked: 'we both understand that in different ways, but play it your way, do as you feel, it can go like that as well',[52] while another student, Georges Mathias, reported that 'Chopin, performer of genius, interpreted Mozart, Beethoven *with the feeling of Chopin*, and it was extremely beautiful, it was sublime'.[53] In other words, Chopin himself translated the works of other composers into his own musical language, achieving a degree of conviction necessary for 'authentic' performance but without imposing himself on the music.

Striking a balance between personal conviction and fidelity to the composer is one prerequisite to successful performance, which can occur only when its constituent parts 'add up' to a coherent conception, to a hierarchy of temporally defined musical gestures ranging from the smallest level of progression to the large-scale controlling shape.[54] This is why some performers fail to convince: put simply, their interpretations do not 'add up', instead suffering from gratuitous effect or incompatibility between, say, the successive elements of poetry and display. Moreover, they evince little or no understanding of the performance aesthetic necessary for the music to make sense, for its expressive vocabulary to speak the composer's language. Typical 'infractions' in the case of Chopin's concertos include sluggish tempos that sap the music of energy and impulse; a hard-edged piano tone inimical to the *bel canto* cantabile favoured by Chopin; overblown or underplayed orchestral backdrops; and wilful, illogical rubato at odds with the composer's controlled shaping of musical time.

For instance, the temporal flexibility of Alexander Brailowsky's Op. 11 from 1928 seems arbitrary, his rubato appropriate only in the Rondo, where the left hand plays in time under the right hand's scherzando give-and-take. Elsewhere, massive cadential ritardandos and accelerated virtuosic sections undermine the performance's logic, likewise meretricious *fioriture* and a jocular cadenza. His 1957 rendition is temporally more coherent, but, paradoxically, it lacks a sense of improvisatory freedom. Both recordings pare down the opening tutti, as does Moriz Rosenthal's, which, less typically, also cuts the Romance's introduction and orchestral transitions in the Rondo. Despite some sensitive pianism, Rosenthal explodes in a massive 'con forza' at bar 56 of the Romance after deliciously light *fioriture* moments earlier, also pounding notes in the Rondo's otherwise deft 'finale' (which, incidentally, features Tausig's variants in bars 512–15).

Nevertheless, his interpretation is preferable to Josef Hofmann's, whose first movement has no *raison d'être*: *fioriture* are showy, quiet themes cocky, gossamer figuration rendered boisterously. Artur Rubinstein's style is more agreeable if ill-conceived in his various readings of Op. 11 and Op. 21. His tone is always cantabile, never harsh, but he depends too heavily on it, skating over the music and its deeper emotion. In contrast, John Barbirolli's orchestra in the 1937 performance conveys a depth of character, as in the last bar of the Allegro maestoso, played with a tragic, intense quality at odds with Rubinstein's casual approach.

The orchestra in Friedrich Gulda's recording employs Balakirev's reinstrumentation, its enriched colours, added countermelodies and reworked articulation (such as pizzicato within the first tutti, versus Chopin's legato indications) masking inconsistencies within the pianistic conception. In the opening movement's second solo, for instance, a slow, introspective thematic statement gives way to an over-fast development section, and the emotional climax at bars 605ff. is equally driven. Dinu Lipatti's interpretation, in contrast, is logical and integrated, framed by portentous octaves and swirls of pianistic colour. He treats the main theme of the Allegro maestoso as an entity, not as concatenated figurations, using the episode thereafter to recharge energy while saving himself for later. Only with the return of the second theme – in which the mood entirely differs from the earlier statement's – does his passion overflow, tinged by a sense of inner tragedy, the movement's conclusion neither fast nor lightweight but sombre and pensive. The Romance is also beautifully shaped, the reprise in bar 80 like a rediscovery, the cadenza a moment of loss.

In Hanna Czerny-Stefańska's performance (formerly attributed to Lipatti), nothing is overstated, each element instead contributing to an all-embracing emotional trajectory. The orchestral playing, although offhand in the opening tutti (which for once is uncut), complements her refined pianism, especially in the Romance, where a reverential tone is created in the introduction, the bassoon intimately engaging with the piano later at bars 80ff. Raoul Koczalski's interpretation is also outstanding, noteworthy for its Chopinesque ornamentation,[55] expressive virtuosity, rich contrasts and variegated textures that maximally exploit the colouristic potential of both hands. Despite the overslow tempos, his performance conception quintessentially suits the music – and is thus far more satisfying than his Op. 21, which, though exemplary at times, is relatively noncommittal. Equally detached is Fou Ts'ong's Op. 11, a sepia performance despairing in tone. His emotional strategy works only occasionally. In the Romance, for instance, the cadenza marks a turning point: once freed of the theme, he plays less secretively, as if released from a burden. In the Rondo, however, a lack of contrast stifles the performance, his participation in the triumphant final chords (scored for orchestra alone) sounding absurd.

Adam Harasiewicz's first movement is also forlorn and his Rondo theme deadpan, while his Romance is cack-handed, some abruptly rolled chords especially incongruous after the tender melody. Still, his rendition is better than Mieczysław Horszowski's drive-through performance or Garrick Ohlsson's saccharine Romance, its mawkishness shattered by a punched-out melody. Krystian Zimerman also plays metallically, as does Bella Davidovich, who pedantically counts the Rondo's 'finale' and injects gratuitous touches. Her reading seems polished, however, compared with Rosina Lhévinne's, while Emmanuel Ax's labours under a Philadelphia Orchestra particularly elephantine in the Rondo.

Infinitely more inspired is the orchestral sound of Claudio Abbado, who with Marta Argerich creates one of the best interpretations on record. Emotionally rich, timbrally varied and rhythmically shaped, the instrumental playing perfectly complements Argerich's consummate pianism, which allows the music to speak for itself in a performance where everything indeed 'adds up'. Maurizio Pollini's playing is nearly as captivating, projecting desperation and confidence alike.

All in all, Lipatti's, Czerny-Stefańska's, Argerich's and Pollini's interpretations of Op. 11 emerge as successful by the criteria defined above, and of these the third is probably best, given the symbiotic partnership between piano and orchestra. It is therefore astonishing that Argerich's Op. 21 is so inept – in part the fault of Mstislav Rostropovich, whose orchestral tuttis are huge and intrusive, while the piano plays mere passagework, with a strident tone to boot. Hofmann's Op. 21, by contrast, is more convincing than his Op. 11, its contrapuntal conception texturally rich and gesturally broad. Duets between piano and orchestra are well handled in the outer movements, while in the Larghetto he logically builds towards the recitative, played with a sombre tone until the mood and colour change at the optimistic trill in bar 70. Stefan Askenase's interpretation is also supremely musical. In the Maestoso's third solo, for instance, his phrases unite in a vocally, even chorally conceived passage where individual parts almost literally speak. Likewise the rapid 'passagework' has a distinct melodic and rhythmic identity, despite being played *sotto voce*, in Chopinesque fashion.

Less successful are the recordings of Marguerite Long and Guiomar Novaes, despite passages of beauty and refinement. Although much of the first movement in Long's 1930 rendition effortlessly sparkles, her kittenish *fioriture* and playful episode at bars 151ff. spoil the mood, while an over-urgent cadenza ruins her flexible, speech-like playing in the recitative. Appalling orchestral ensemble exacerbates matters, although at least the accompaniment is Chopin's, whereas her 1955 recording uses Messager's orchestration. Here the pianist must play *con forza* to compete with the brassy orchestra, its earlier sheen dulled by a mechanical tone, declamatory flexibility lapsing into rhythmic distortion. Although extraordinarily slow, Novaes's first movement is perhaps closer to Chopin's intentions thanks to its contrapuntal conception and emotional shape, but her Larghetto almost loses the will to live and her

Allegro vivace is utterly humourless (and thus like Zimerman's Brahms-ian reading of the work).

Clara Haskil's interpretation is no less stifled, her polite, nuance-free playing making the huge interjections in Cortot's reorchestrated accompaniment seem unbalanced. Cortot's own recording works better, thanks to his closer rapport with the orchestra. In the Maestoso, for instance, the instrumental accompaniment fully participates in the interpretation (especially in the development section), and in other movements dialogues with the soloist enhance the spirit of partnership. Cortot's temporal flexibility is especially refined in the slow movement, where certain figurations are shaped with the 'accelerando principle',[56] and in bars 169–76 of the Allegro vivace, where delayed notes effect the 'national rubato' central to Chopin's style. Other Chopinesque features include colouristic washes, effortless *fioriture*, 'vital' tempos and dynamic contrasts, all of which mitigate the occasionally jarring accents and sloppy articulation.

Vladimir Ashkenazy's performance is more consistently excellent, the orchestra again acting as partner to the piano, which sounds polished and passionate. A bit more emotion might have suited the Larghetto, likewise the rhythmic flexibility so fundamental to a vocal rather than instrumental conception. The recitative in particular is too even, killing the music's speech-like character, but the cadenza and gorgeous reprise more than compensate, the latter featuring a reminiscent piano and bassoon duet *aus der Ferne*. Not until the last movement, however, does the interpretation come into its own, Ashkenazy's light, quiet touch complemented by left-hand impulses exploiting Chopin's dance-derived rhythms.

Murray Perahia's recording also excels in technical polish and conceptual logic. His sound is liquid and colouristically rich, enhanced by Zubin Mehta's variegated orchestral timbres, although here again the recitative is too measured (perhaps in order to avoid sentimentality) while the 'passagework' in the outer movements hurries by. But his playing is always controlled – in contrast to Melvyn Tan's lamentable 'period' performance, which only proves that an 'original' instrument[57] is no interpretative panacea. His first movement is rushed and amorphous, the Larghetto's *fioriture* brittle, the Allegro vivace's rhythmic impulse stifled by an inert left hand. There is more to praise timbrally, particularly in the third-movement's 'finale', where he deploys the *una corda* for delicacy of sound (or perhaps to mask wrong notes). Roger Norrington too coaxes lovely colours from the orchestra, but his tempos are rigidly fast – in short, as offensive as the randomly variable ones from earlier in the century. Fumiko Shiraga's performances of both concertos with quintet accompaniment create a more plausible 'period' atmosphere, even though she uses a modern piano. By playing in the tutti passages – as Chopin himself might have done – Shiraga adds weight to the accompaniment and compensates for the wind cues missing from Op. 21's string parts (for instance, the third movement's 'Cor de signal'). But an abruptness in the ornamentation (performed before the beat), the artificial boosting of the quintet on the recording and the use of the 'artist's [i.e. Shiraga's] manuscripts' as the basis of the accompaniment undermine the sense of hearing Chopin's concertos as he played them.

Of course, that distance from the original impairs virtually all the recordings of Op. 11 and Op. 21 included in this survey, few of which evoke 'the feeling of Chopin' by calling upon the performance aesthetic so vital to their compositional conception and first incarnations in 'living sound'. And thus, despite the huge weight of interpretation already resting upon the concertos, a further attempt will be made in Chapter 4 to reinterpret and re-evaluate the two works – this time, in so far as possible, 'in the spirit of their creator'.[58]

4

Re-evaluation

Principles and premises

Music thrives on a tension between its elemental temporal progression and the structural frameworks that lend it shape and coherence. It was observed in Chapter 3 that the opposed yet interdependent elements creating this tension have variously attracted the attention of scholars and listeners over the ages: at times music's diachronic, 'narrative' flow has been privileged in critical writing, at others its synchronic, synoptic organisation, while recently a more reconciliatory approach has been taken in the literature. The symbiotic relationship between narrative and architecture – one continually and necessarily exploited by performers – is what will guide the analytical re-evaluation of Chopin's concertos to follow here. I shall first define each movement's skeletal structure, identifying important 'stabilising' features such as tonal scheme and sectional form, and then in tracing through the music I shall observe temporally defined processes like the generation and relaxation of momentum, rhythmic flux, and small- and large-scale gestural impulse, all of which help to transform the structural bedrock into a living musical statement.[1] In this way, an understanding will be gained of the continual give-and-take between the music's underlying foundation and its unfolding progression, between all-embracing structures and the here-and-now. The theories of Schenker[2] and others will be invoked as required along the way, and the particularly 'vital' responses to the concertos of Fink, Stoepel, Lenz, Merkel and Kretschmar used as points of departure in an attempt to resuscitate works that make sense not as inanimate objects but only when brought to life in sound.[3]

bar:	1	37	75	101	125	151	181	206	225	252	257	269	273	301	337–48
thematic group/ section:	1, 2		1	epi-sode 1	2	epi-sode 2	( )		devel-opment			1	2	episode 3/ 'finale' (≈episode 2)	
tutti/ solo:	T_1		S_1				T_2 S_2				T_3	S_3			T_4
main key:	i (F minor)		→$^b/_{III}$	III (A♭ major)	v - - - - v (C minor)		III→iv→$V^{6---5}_{4---\natural}$ (C major)				i (F minor)	III→V i			i

Figure 4.1 Op. 21, i: form and tonal plan

Op. 21, Maestoso

Form and tonal plan

Op. 21's first movement follows the conventional succession of alternating tutti and solo sections described in Chapter 1 (see Figure 4.1). The opening tutti starts in the tonic F minor with theme 1a, moving through the mediant A♭ major with a statement of the second theme and reaching the dominant after the piano's arresting entry on a diminished harmony in bar 71. S_1 follows a similar plan, progressing from F minor (in which two themes – 1a and 1b – are stated, the latter heard only once in the piece, played by the piano) through the second theme's A♭ major to C minor, the dominant minor, which is lengthily prolonged until T_2 begins in bar 181. After an interrupted cadence, the piano re-enters playing a variant of theme 1a in A♭ major at bar 206, with B♭ minor (iv; bars 221–30) and the dominant C major the principal keys to follow in the development section proper, although embedded within considerable sequential activity (detailed later). The brief T_3 stays in V until the recapitulation starts at bar 269. Here Chopin remains close to F minor, moving from theme 1a directly to the second theme (again in A♭ major, in somewhat unorthodox fashion), but back to the tonic via the dominant by bar 301. It is of course in the tonic that T_4 closes the movement nearly fifty bars later. Thus the Maestoso rests upon three versions of a simple progression from the tonic through the mediant to the dominant: in the exposition, the goal harmony is the dominant minor; in the development, the dominant major; in the recapitulation, the tonic.[4] Each iteration supports a variety of often complex harmonies at the more immediate levels discussed below.

Narrative

The harmonic outline also supports an emotional unfolding of astonishing depth and subtlety for a composer of only nineteen years. Chopin transcends his models while clearly drawing upon them. Obvious commonalities include the use of dotted rhythms in the opening melody; non-recurrent orchestral themes thereafter instead of the pianistic one heard later in the exposition; solo right-hand lead-ins to the second theme; varied restatements of the opening theme at the start of S_2 and abbreviated recapitulations thereof in T_3; and, in S_3, reworked transpositions of the first solo's concluding material, rather than a separate 'finale'. But the many differences are of greater import, among them the natural lie of Chopin's figuration as opposed to the immensely difficult virtuosity in Hummel's Op. 85; Op. 21's expressive integration, opposite in effect from the mismatched moods in Hummel's Op. 89 and Kalkbrenner's Op. 61; and the solid tonal and sectional logic of the Chopin movement, versus the formal sprawl of Field's A♭ major.

When played at or near the designated ♩ = 138,[5] the first tutti in Op. 21 is taut and exciting, forward impulse being controlled by four principal rhythmic ideas and exploitation of the statement–response pattern that Chopin inherited from Mozart.[6] The angular melody and bass descent in the first four bars give way to a developmental 'sentence' (1 + 1 + 2 bars) achieving a climax at *ff* only seconds after the opening *p*. Momentum is more gradually increased thereafter through syncopated and repeated-quaver rhythms which build towards bar 19's eruption, the temperature then kept high for some twelve bars. Chopin starts to wind down in bar 31 in preparation for the second theme's entrance six bars later; marked 'dolce e legato' in his piano reduction (but not the orchestral parts), this is kept simple to avoid competition with the soloist's statement thereof later on. After some inconsequential motivic play in bars 55–8, the crotchet/four-semiquaver melody and processional repeated-quaver accompaniment from bar 17 return, now harnessed to achieve a final climax before six bars of retraction (not least in the harmonic rhythm) towards the pianist's dramatic entrance in bar 71.

The announcement (*Eingang*) is concise and theme 1a follows at once, distinct in character from the standard *stile brillante* introductory melody. Initially similar to the orchestral version, the piano's 1a explodes at bar 81 in an impassioned *fioritura* ('con forza', with a break indicated in Dubois' score after the top A♭) that heralds the emotional turbulence of the ensuing theme 1b, also unveiling the pianistic style that will dominate the solo sections. The new theme, heard for the first time, is breathtaking when performed with the finesse of touch and colouristic nuance that Chopin himself mastered. Combining *fioritura* elaborations of the simple melodic outline, contrapuntal textures (note especially the poignant alto and tenor countermelodies in Example 4.1), and octave

Example 4.1 Op. 21, i: theme 1b (bars 82–91[1])

doublings (marked 'stretto' in bar 89, by which Chopin literally means 'tightened' or intensified, not 'accelerando'), the first half of theme 1b is in a sentence structure – 2 + 2 + 4 bars – and forms a period with the second half, which takes a different turning in bar 94. Here momentum increases as do registral and dynamic ranges,[7] a climax occurring in bars 99–100 with the dissonant right-hand elaboration of a left-hand diminished harmony. With the dominant in bar 101, semiquaver activity seamlessly takes over at the point where a *Spielepisode* would have commenced in most virtuoso concertos. Chopin's approach, in contrast, is innovative and subtle: short and long gestures, tiny melodic fragments, catapulting arpeggio figurations, and clashing dissonances propel the music with increasing fervour back to the dominant in bar 115, whereupon a celebratory modulation to the relative major begins. Here some of the most glorious writing in the movement pours out, in a passage which seems 'transitional' but contains tantalising tenor countermelodies over a simple bass foundation, while the right hand floats across the keyboard in deliciously convoluted patterns before briefly settling in bars 121–2 (the suspended minim f[2]s waiting to resolve in bar 123) and then preparing the second theme with the decorated arpeggio alluded to earlier.[8]

Announced in T_1, the new theme forms an extended period over eighteen bars (4 + 4, 4 + 2 + 4), reaching an interrupted cadence in bar 142 that provokes a recitative-like effusion of incredible intensity. Before that, Chopin combines angular patterns with a liquid *fioritura* in bar 127 and other *bel canto*-inspired ornamentation such as bar 132's rolled chord (the lowest note, ab^1, to be played on the beat, followed by $d\natural^2$, g^2 and f^2, according to notation in Dubois' score), all over an 'exploratory' left-hand accompaniment of considerable textural variety. With the increase in energy in bars 139–40, the music reaches what seems to be a concluding passage in bars 141–2, whereupon a *Spielepisode* in the prevailing Ab major would logically follow (perhaps employing figuration like that heard at bars 161ff.). But Chopin defies expectations with an even more 'vocal' passage alternating between a slow descending motive (compare the cadential descents in bars 84, 86, 92, 126, 128, 134 and 136) and flourishes often highly chromatic and dissonant in nature which rapidly change register over a more contained, portentous left hand. The mood quickly shifts to one of struggle and despair (note bar 149's 'con duolo' cadence, after an exhausted *leggierissimo* descent through two-and-a-half octaves), the passage's effect all the more powerful given its unpredictability.[9]

After this expressive peak, Chopin gradually restores momentum in a section of the utmost refinement antithetical to the rollicking episodes of Kalkbrenner *et al.* A succession of closed two-bar units reinforcing the dominant minor cadence leads via an ascending fifths progression to a tentative but lyrical extension and ultimately to bar 161's surprise return of Ab major, here as VI of C minor.[10] For the next eight bars and beyond the figuration is once again ravishing, initially contained within two-bar gestures but inspiring broader sweeps of sound – a typical process throughout the concertos, as we shall see. Note the textural richness of bars 161–2, the simple left-hand accompaniment supporting an upper-line stepwise descent and a zigzagging arpeggio in the middle, then four insistent f^2–eb^2 motions with a syncopated cadential descent above. The counterpoint is even more ingenious in bars 165–6 and 167–8, with dialogues between the upper parts featuring expressive suspensions and appoggiaturas. As excitement mounts (the pervasive dotted rhythm returning in bar 169), Chopin deftly turns to C minor in bars 171–2, and the rest of the section builds towards the definitive cadence in that key after the obligatory trill in bars 179–80, doubled a sixth below with a framing tremolo played by the right hand's outer fingers.

T_2 remains at fever pitch until fragments of theme 1b enter at *p* in bars 188 and 190, interspersed with references to theme 1a. Tension quickly rises, due to the repeated-quaver and dotted rhythms in bars 192ff. After the climax, a more definitive retraction occurs in bar 199 before the piano's entrance six bars later, in anticipation of which the flutes and clarinets play a fragment from theme 1a, answered by the bassoon's dolorous restatement of theme 2 material. The tutti ends with the same 'deceptive' progression as in bars 160–1, from V^7 of C minor to A♭ major.

At this point the piano returns with the major-key version of theme 1a, played in octaves sequentially restated a key higher.[11] A flurry of figuration in bars 214–16 leads to a nocturne-like 'improvisation' reminiscent of bars 143–8 and loosely affiliated with themes 1b and 2, although the mood is hushed and expectant, as if waiting for the development section proper to begin in bar 225, in V of iv (as in Op. 11's Allegro maestoso). Successive sequential progressions predominate once Chopin moves away from B♭ minor, with circle-of-fifths and then 'harmonic appoggiatura' patterns in bars 233–40. The rather exposed G minor in bar 241 provokes a linear ascent in the bass featuring C minor in first inversion (bar 243), F minor (bar 245) and G♭ major (bar 247), which launches a last, chromatic sequence to the second-inversion dominant at bar 252. All the while the right hand indulges in fast and furious virtuosity, inscribing up-and-down arcs made up largely of embellished arpeggio shapes; non-developmental in and of itself, the keyboard passagework is offset by orchestral treatment of the principal thematic material (especially theme 1a). This is structurally the least cogent part of the movement, the concatenated sequences and deluge of notes undermining the music's forward progression.[12] Nevertheless, balanced phrase structures and the terrific build-up of momentum with the chromatic ascents in bars 249ff. generate a goal-directed impetus further reinforced by the cascading chromatic descent in thirds[13] to the dominant that ushers in T_3 in bar 257.

For ten bars the orchestra plays with unbridled intensity at the movement's peak of energy, the dominant forcefully articulated as the overriding harmonic goal thus far. It is therefore surprising that F minor's return, achieved with the piano's restatement of theme 1a in bars 268ff., is so short-lived. Almost immediately the recapitulation is abandoned and theme 2 re-enters in A♭ major, eliding the haunting theme 1b of such expressive potency in the exposition (this substitution nevertheless confirming the affinity between themes 1b and 2). Initially accompanied by a horn pedal on eb^1, the second theme is virtually as before apart from exquisite new embellishments in bars 273 and 275, and five evocative db^2-eb^2 dyads in bar 279 which only eventually resolve as expected. But in bar 290 Chopin sidesteps the interrupted cadence from before and launches another 'improvisatory' outpouring featuring right-hand *fioriture* and other shapes over left-hand chord-outlining patterns,[14] in a surge of energy reinforcing F minor as tonic. Though less intense than the recitative in bars 143–50 (it could hardly be more so), the passage effectively seals the recapitulation, and what follows sounds like a 'finale'. It is however the material from bars 151ff., transposed up a fourth and almost identical to its earlier counterpart, although different in feel if no less pianistically satisfying. The 'con forza' at bar 322 ends the reprise of this passage, moving headlong into an extended, harmonically accelerated build-up to the second-inversion dominant at bar 331 that ultimately resolves to T_4's emphatic downbeat tonic by means of another trill complex. The movement's defiant close occurs after six more bars at *f* or *ff* and a final statement of the ubiquitous theme 1a, with a cadential variant of the statement–response pattern from bars 4–7 leading to the end.

If the fluctuating levels of intensity throughout the movement were graphically traced, climaxes would be noted within each of the four tuttis (the economy of which paradoxically enhances the dialogue effect between piano and orchestra) and, especially, towards the end of the exposition, development and recapitulation sections. These are countered by more reflective passages sometimes anguished in tone (for instance, theme 1b and the 'recitative' following theme 2), the sense of coherence being reinforced by the complementary nature of the material and by the incontrovertible logic of Chopin's emotional argument. In contrast to the virtuoso concertos of Hummel and others, this Maestoso forges vital links between the different resources at Chopin's disposal – piano and orchestra, poetry and display. As observed earlier, an innate equilibrium is thus recovered from the Mozart piano concerto,[15] a balance between parts and whole and between structure and narrative that has ensured the movement's vigour and appeal to the present day.

bar:	1	7 15 26 34	45 58 66 72	75 83	91–7
subsection:		a_1 b_1 a_2 c	r_1 r_2 r_3 ⌢	a_3 b_2	
section:	introduction	A	B (recitative)	A'	coda
main key:	I	I	i	I	I
	(A♭ major)		(A♭ minor)	(A♭ major)	

Figure 4.2 Op. 21, ii: form and tonal plan

Op. 21, Larghetto

Form and tonal plan

The slow movement (at ♩ = 56) has a simple ternary outline – A, B, A' – with a brief orchestral statement serving as both introduction and coda (in each case, a piano flourish ends the passage). Tonally the movement is also straightforward, a progression from the tonic A♭ major through the parallel A♭ minor back to A♭ major spanning the three principal sections. Within the outer two, Chopin generally stays close to the tonic and dominant, whereas section B's recitative is more wide-ranging, progressing from A♭ minor through C♭ major (♭III, bar 58) and the subdominant minor (bar 62) to the dominant (bar 66). This prevails until A' commences in bar 75, after a short fermata-cum-cadenza. The breakdown in Figure 4.2 summarises the movement.

Narrative

Within this outline Chopin pours the most liquid cantabile writing yet to flow from his pen. The effusive 'ornamental melody' for which he became renowned colours sections A and A', while the recitative's melodic embellishment assumes a dramatic rather than lyrical role. Comparison with Chopin's models reveals the spontaneity and originality of his figuration. Nearly all the slow movements in the five concertos that most influenced him – Hummel Opp. 85 and 89, Moscheles Op. 58, Kalkbrenner Op. 61, and Field A♭ major – follow ternary plans, only Field's lacking an orchestral introduction. In three of them, the piano

Example 4.2 Op. 21, ii: thematic incipits, sections A and B

enters alone thereafter, and in four the left hand strums a nocturne-like accompaniment in arpeggios or repeated chords while the right hand intones a cantilena melody registrally removed from the lower part. Operatic gestures abound, not least 'vocal' ornaments, short cadenzas at fermatas and, especially in Moscheles' Op. 58,[16] recitative textures. But in each case, notwithstanding passages of remarkable beauty, Chopin's achievement is emotionally more profound and musically more satisfying – far more so than its putative inspiration, his adolescent infatuation for Konstancja Gładkowska, might lead one to expect.

The opening dialogue between strings and winds ends with the piano's resonant arpeggio to $e\flat^1$, followed by a linear motion to the appoggiatura-like flourish from c^2, which, according to the liaison in Dubois' score, should begin on the downbeat (see Example 4.2), just as the ensuing $d\natural^3$ should sound with the left hand's third-beat chord. This sinuous 'ornamental melody', initially outlined in the tenor part, articulates a simple descent from E♭ through C and B♭ to A♭, echoing the strings in bars 1–2 and confirming a motive ('x') of later importance as well. But of greater note is the sheer plasticity of line and rhythm, the textural variety, and the consummate control of register. Equally impressive is Chopin's contrapuntal technique, especially his alto and tenor parts, shared between the hands in bar 9 (the third-beat $a\natural^1$, played simultaneously with the left hand's B♭, moves to $g\flat^1$ on beat 4) and then merged into a single voice doubling the melodic line above, which descends over an octave from the $d\flat^3$ in bar 9 to bar 13's c^2 and $b\flat^1$. After reaching V in bar 14, Chopin introduces a simpler melody in octaves, with canonic touches below (subsection b_1). Anticipations of Op. 11's Romance (especially its bar 15) occur here, likewise at the decorated cadential descent in thirds in bar 21, marked '*pp*' in Dubois. Before this, a warm D♭ major harmony enters in bar 19 presaging later use of the subdominant in bars 34ff., the recitative and section A'; the successive rolled articulations soften the chordal attacks, achieving smooth contours despite the relatively slow rhythms. But within moments the right hand launches an incredibly labile prolongation of the dominant soaring to new registral heights only to plunge at bar 24's 'con forza'. Chopin ceaselessly varies colour and shape, the tenor countermelody stabilising the discursive upper part.

Bar 25's exultant V leads back to the opening melody (compare its anacrusis to bar 6's; once again the right-hand c^2 is linked to the left-hand A♭ in Dubois), newly embellished by gorgeous *fioriture* respectively marked 'delicatissimo', '*f*', 'leggierissimo' and 'dolcissimo' in bars 26, 28, 30 and 31. Other differences between subsections a_1 and a_2 range from the captivating syncopations in bar 27 and languorous c^2s in bar 32 to bar 28's sudden flare of passion, surprisingly vehement after the prevailing tranquillity. This change of atmosphere anticipates the darker shadows of bars 37ff., after the new direction taken with bar 34's fervent tonicisation of IV (note bar 35's *ff*) in subsection c. The key then shifts to A♭ minor in a highly expressive passage (Chopin indicates 'staccato', 'raddolcendo', 'stringendo', '*f*', '*p*', 'smorzando' and numerous hairpins within five bars) which concludes section A and leads in a terrific crescendo of dramatic tension to the recitative, prepared by forceful piano flourishes in dialogue with orchestral interjections (the winds playing in bars 44–5 for only the second time since bar 5).

A stylised *recitativo accompagnato* or *stromentato*, the new section employs a technique used in the Maestoso, namely an alternation between slow melodic shapes (usually crotchet appoggiaturas) and rapid flourishes ideally brought to life with the 'accelerando principle' essential to their vocal character.[17] Doubled in octaves (like Moscheles' recitative textures), the *appassionato* melody initially restates the motive underlying section A's theme ('x' – see Example 4.2) but altered to E♭–C♭–B♭–A♭, and then proceeds in short or long utterances over the tremolo accompaniment admired by Tovey,[18] which over thirteen bars articulates a linear descent (A♭–G–G♭–F♭–E♭) typical of Chopin's improvisatory music. The piano part above this foundation is extraordinarily intense, exploring registral and dynamic extremes in the *fioriture* interspersing the long appoggiaturas, the former recalling similar shapes in the outer sections (compare for instance bar 8, beats 3–4, and the second half of bar 47). In bars 50–1 the sequentially higher melodic restatement proceeds to an increasingly agitated extension (characterised by more frequent crotchet appoggiaturas and marked 'sempre più stretto' from bar 54) culminating in a cadence on V after bar 56's registral peak at *ff*. The modulatory deflection to C♭ major that follows is operatic in nature, launching a new phase within the recitative (r_2) more confident but still nostalgic in tone. Initially 'sotto voce', the comparatively confined melody branches out after bar 61's sequential transposition. Here ascending scales and descending arpeggios lead via a final melisma ('con forza') to bar 66's structural dominant, whereupon r_3 begins. This concluding phase is tinged by loss and regret, due to the slower rhythms, the restatements of motive x straddling bars 66–7 and 67–8, and the solemn horn octaves on E♭ in bars 68–70, which accompany a last, exhausted *fioritura* in bar 69. But the flutes and clarinets in bar 70 inject new optimism, as do the piano's trills over the next few bars. After the rapid scale in bar 72, the soloist plays a brief but kaleidoscopic 'cadenza' – in fact, an extension of the fermata from 72,[19] its D♭ resolving only on the downbeat of bar 75 after the *dolcissimo* sequential descent outlining a major scale from bar 73's first-inversion A♭ chord to the cadence an octave lower.

The opening melody's return further dispels accrued tensions, although violent passions erupt in the cathartic flourish of bar 77, which unleashes repeated notes, turning figures, arpeggios, chromatic lines and reaching-over shapes within four quavers. After bar 78's restoration of normal rhythmic activity, the poignantly simple triplet semiquavers in bar 79 lead to bar 80's celebratory effusion, remarkable for its varied rhythm, contour and articulation[20] – all of which testify to the young Chopin's mastery and originality of keyboard technique. The more elaborate bars 81–2 proceed to a subsection b_2 almost identical to its earlier counterpart, except that Chopin crystallises the soloist's suggestive canon into an initially antiphonal bassoon countermelody accompanying the piano through its warmer, more processive approach to the *appassionato* bars 89–90. Here the right hand ascends in thirds over a left-hand second-inversion dominant disposed as in bar 7, with a tenor countermelody penetrating the wash of colour that accumulates as the bar progresses (characteristically, the pedal is held throughout). At the peak of the two-bar arch – surprisingly, marked '*pp*' in Dubois – the figuration turns chromatic in the lower right-hand part, implicitly slurred from the second semiquaver in each group to the first in the next, while the upper line picks out a diminished arpeggio subtly recalling the A♭ minor harmony of section B. Reinforced by the horns, the cadence is of course to A♭ major; the introductory material then returns as a coda, the piano closing the movement with an A♭ arpeggio.

Verbal description can hardly do justice to this exquisite 'tone poem', in which extremes of emotion are expertly juxtaposed as in Chopin's nocturnes. In fact, in everything but name the Larghetto is a nocturne – appropriately so, given that the nocturne genre had its origins as a vocal serenade and that Chopin apparently intended the movement as a tribute to Konstancja. But it is far more than a testament to his youthful devotion. The Larghetto's unsentimental expressivity (at least when performed 'in his spirit') and the astounding invention and combination of keyboard figuration have secured the movement's place not only within the concert canon but also among the finest music that Chopin ever composed.

Op. 21, Allegro vivace

Form and tonal plan

The Allegro vivace can be interpreted as either a symmetrical ternary form (like Chopin's earlier mazurkas) or a goal-directed structure influenced by the sonata principle. Despite obvious similarities to his *Rondo à la mazur* Op. 5 and other works in the genre, the movement is not in

bar:	1	65	141	197	325	405	494–514
material:	theme 1		themes 2a, 2b, 2c, 2d	development	theme 1+ development	f_1, f_2; f_1, f_3	c_1, c_2, c_3
section:	A	episode 1	B	episode 2	A′	'finale'	coda
main key:	i (F minor)	i → $^V/_{III}$	III (A♭ major)	→ V	i (F minor)	I (F major)	I

Figure 4.3 Op. 21, iii: form and tonal plan

rondo form,[21] instead comprising only three principal thematic sections – A, B and A′, respectively in the tonic (F minor), relative major (A♭ major) and tonic – separated by episodic passages and followed by a bravura 'finale' and coda in the parallel F major. Another difference can be seen in the second episode, which participates in one of the 'dynamic' structures that Chopin started exploiting around this time, namely, the i → III → V → i progression (bars 1–325) also used in the first movement. Furthermore, episode 2 – by far the longest section – has a developmental function, elaborating both the opening theme and the fourfold thematic complex introduced in section B.[22] Thus Chopin achieves a formal hybrid uniting the thematic statements and episodes into a single sweep towards the 'finale' and coda (see Figure 4.3).

Narrative

The soloist starts the movement with a poignant melody (theme 1, at ♩. = 69) tracing the up-and-down arc typical of the Polish mazur over a contrapuntal left-hand accompaniment. In various ways the opening resembles that of the third movement in Hummel's Op. 85 (especially its bittersweet, folk-inspired theme, played by the piano); other features – not least the Lydian fourth – recall Chopin's own *Rondo à la mazur*. Mazurka-like variation prevails in section A and indeed throughout the movement,[23] especially within the thrice-stated theme 1, its first and third bars continually undergoing change (compare bars 1, 9 and 25, and bars 3, 11 and 27) in part by the injection of chromaticism and other ornamentation. Chromaticism also colours the responses to the initial four-bar unit within each thematic statement, especially the third of these, much extended and sinuously propelling the music towards the tutti's concluding passage in bars 45–64, which contains a lengthy cadence (bars 45–52) plus two codas (bars 53–60, 61–4). Other borrowings from the mazurka genre include hemiolas and syncopations (particularly second-beat accents, for instance in the tutti interjection in bars 16–24); an obsessive manipulation of small cells (as in bars 33–6 and the orchestra's conclusion in bars 45ff.); and 'motivic' use of the up-and-down contour (compare theme 1 and bars 41–4, 45–9, 49–53 etc.). The energy created by juxtaposed ascents and descents is one reason why the music sounds so effortless, thanks also to the momentum of phrase structure mastered by Chopin in earlier dance pieces.[24]

After the orchestral cadence, the piano's *fortissimo* 'announcement' in bars 65ff. – a device also used in Hummel Op. 89, Moscheles Op. 58 and, especially, Kalkbrenner Op. 61 – picks up from where the soloist left off in bar 44, introducing two rhythmic features important hereafter: triplet quavers and a five-crotchet idea (♩ ♩ ♩ | ♩ ♩ 𝄽) on which Chopin bases much of episode 1. The latter begins in earnest after two sequential down–up patterns reversing section A's melodic arc and recalling the orchestra's arpeggiation in bars 49–50. From bar 81 an exuberant right-hand melody in triplet quavers traces a series of tortuous up-and-down shapes over eight bars (divided 2 + 2 + 4, the last of which is a momentum-building extension), while the left hand intones a lilting countermelody derived from the five-note idea in bars 69–70 and 77–8, and clarinets, flutes and bassoons engage in canonic dialogues also echoing this shape. Moving through sequentially related keys – A♭ major (III), D♭ major (VI) and B♭ minor (iv), with a developmental circle-of-fifths progression to the last of these – the successive melodic statements finally reach the dominant minor, C minor, after which a furious ascent in both hands (starting in F minor) provokes a cascade of triplet quavers before the more sedate orchestral conclusion, in which fragments of the first theme appear between antiphonal wind commentaries.

The brief orchestral introduction to the second thematic group begins in bar 141, violins playing *col legno* while violas and cellos strum syncopated *bourdon* fifths deriving, like the implied hemiolas above, from the mazurka genre.[25] As in other works from the period,[26] the oberek-inspired melody – theme 2a in Figure 4.3 – is presented in octaves; it also features second- and third-beat accents, the Lydian fourth, and hemiola sub-groupings. Marked 'scherzando', the theme has a periodic construction (8 + 8), initially outlines a motivically important arpeggio shape in triplet quavers and ends with a four-bar conclusion to be played with Chopin's 'national rubato' – that is, with rhythmic flexibility in the solo part, against a steady orchestral backdrop. Theme 2b sets in immediately in bar 161, its key of A♭ minor, tauter rhythms (based on the ♩ ♩ ♩ │ ♩ ♩ 𝄾 pattern from before) and more confined registral ambit contrasting with the relatively carefree melody beforehand. It is short-lived, however, as yet another theme – 2c, marked 'risvegliato' (awakened, aroused) – enters in bar 169 over a waltz-like accompaniment, employing the Lydian fourth (subtly anticipated by the bassoon in bar 167) and third-beat forzatos analogous to the mazurka's foot-stamping accents. Here again Chopin specifies rubato (bar 173), which prevails even after theme 2d's arrival four bars later. More closural in nature, it features short, snappy rhythmic units in the right hand over a stylised drone in the left (highlighted by the horn's E♭ pedal), the sinuous, *dolcissimo* chromaticism of bars 185ff. leading to a more expansive eight-bar conclusion over a descent to V in the bass (A♭–G♭–F–F♭–E♭). This superbly constructed passage demonstrates Chopin's ability to generate material from tiny cells: as Figure 4.4 shows, the four themes have similar rhythmic profiles, and there are commonalities in pitch as well – for instance, the C–A♭–E♭–E♭ motion underlying both themes 2a and 2c, a parallel exploited later in the movement.

The arpeggiation launching episode 2 emerges naturally from the second-theme complex, as do certain rhythmic ideas (for instance, the ♩ ♪♪♪ ♩ pattern shared by theme 2a and bars 199ff.). Initially built in eight-bar phrases, with responsorial obbligatos from clarinet and bassoon, the music becomes more intense after a descending circle-of-fifths sequence in bars 213ff., which precedes a sequential ascent through an octave outlining a whole-tone scale in bars 221–8 and connecting successive minor harmonies. The left hand controls rhythmic and harmonic flow, supporting an increasingly frenetic, convoluted right-hand motion that inscribes arpeggios continually changing direction. These provoke a more metrically fragmented dissolution of tension noteworthy for its hemiolas and articulation, once again moving through the circle of fifths to bar 235's G♭ major. At this point the right hand

theme 2a	
theme 2b	
theme 2c (second bar)	
theme 2d	
'Cor de signal'	
'finale' theme	

Figure 4.4 Op. 21, iii: rhythmic commonalities

breaks free of the two-crotchet hemiolas in a soaring arpeggio counter-
balanced by downward scales, ultimately reaching a more developmental phase within the episode from bar 245, where the left hand plays
theme 2b underneath an embellished version thereof in the right. After
four bars of suspensive arpeggios in G♭ major, theme 2d appears under a
right-hand trill preparing the delightful bars 261ff., where Chopin verti-
cally juxtaposes theme 2a (left hand) and an embellished theme 2c (right
hand), marked 'risvegliato' as before. This contrapuntal stroke of
genius, which emphasises the thematic complex's compatibility (Figure
4.4), moves steadily through C♭ major, E♭ minor and D♭ major, arriving at
the dominant in bar 285 whereupon Chopin begins his retransition to
the opening theme, to return forty bars later. Before that, the temperature briefly mounts (the tutti's *fortissimo* Cs in bars 291–2 reversing the
now familiar ♩ ♩ ♩ | ♩ ♩ ♪ pattern) but then drops with theme 2a's
subito reappearance in bars 293ff., its focus on C and its 'liquidation', or
progressive fragmentation, gradually stabilising the music.[27] After more
hemiolas, the pace slows as piano and clarinets engage in quiet dialogue,
the former's arpeggiations in C major punctuating the latter's hints of
theme 1, which arrives in earnest after an eight-bar 'coruscating shower

of chromatic particles'[28] played 'leggieramente' and at ppp. Thus closes Chopin's most successful *Spielepisode* yet, thanks to the organic connection and balanced phraseology inspired by his dance models.

The recapitulation proceeds more or less literally until bar 353, where Chopin abruptly interjects a developmental variant of theme 2d 'allowed' by the intersplicing of ideas typical of the mazurka, also exploiting the similarity of the left-hand accompanimental patterns. This brief parenthesis moves through fifths-related harmonies (E♭, A♭^{7}, D♭^{7}, G♭^{7}) to arrive at an intensifying passage over a chromatic ascent in the bass (C♭–C♮–D♭) then inverted in miniature as theme 1 returns, picking up from the counterpart to bar 29. The rest of the section unfolds virtually as before, except that the orchestral conclusion unexpectedly broadens and modulates to F major at ff. Here the movement's main business ends and the 'finale' begins, introduced by an evocative solo horn call[29] echoing the second-theme complex and preparing for the new left-hand melody seconds later, itself allied to themes 2a–d (see again Figure 4.4).

As Figure 4.3 suggests, the 'finale' divides into two parts. The first, comprising f_1 and f_2 (bars 409–24, 425–48), follows a pattern familiar from Chopin's other works in the *stile brillante*, namely, a succession of short units answered by more expansive momentum-generating gestures. The twice-stated eight-bar phrase within f_1 is particularly snappy, with the two hands out of phase by a crotchet while the chromatic line in the right propels the music. Section f_2 is equally electrifying, tension increasing with the eight-bar swell in bars 441–8, which suspends the metre while pushing towards f_1's return in bar 449. Although similar to f_2, f_3 is darker in mood, the bass ascending through successive fourths linked chromatically (F–F♯–G) while the right twists and turns above. As before, parallel diminished sevenths in bars 481–4 cloud the music, clarity returning with the second-inversion dominant in bar 485 – at fff, the movement's peak of energy. After a trill-like configuration in bars 489–90 and tutti response in bars 491–2, the music stops dead in bar 493, the piano entering again one bar later with theme 2d's final statement at p (the coda's first phase, c_1), its nostalgic mood resolving accrued tensions in keeping with the typical sonata-form conclusion. But an explosion occurs with the soloist's cascade of notes at bar 502 (c_2), which is similar to that ending Op. 5 (note especially the Lydian fourths), the register plummeting and then climbing before the orchestra's four punctuating bars (c_3).

Op. 21's Allegro vivace thus demonstrates the young composer's handling of musical impulse, its continual give-and-take and playful tensions carrying the listener from start to finish in perhaps the most seamless flow of ideas to emerge from Chopin thus far. Here the foundation is laid for other large-scale works to come; at the same time, the movement fittingly closes a 'virtuoso concerto' of remarkable originality and rarest quality.

Op. 11, Allegro maestoso

Form and tonal plan

The first movement of Op. 11 resembles its models in many respects, but it is nevertheless highly original. More than any other work by Chopin, it has aroused critical censure for its unorthodox tonal scheme, even though (as we shall see) this contributes to its 'profound effect' in performance. Figure 4.5 depicts the movement's form (compare Figures 1.1 and 4.1), tonal outline and dynamic peaks, the first occurring near the end of episode 1, where Chopin reaches the dominant in preparation for the second theme's entrance in the tonic major, versus the more conventional mediant harmony (shown in the hypothetical key scheme underneath). The tonic prevails until S_2's commencement in C major (VI), after which successive modulations lead to V and the second dynamic peak at bar 478. With T_3 the tonic returns, and only then, during the recapitulation, does the second theme appear in a subsidiary key – G major (III) – followed by the movement's most overtly expressive passage, marked with an asterisk in Figure 4.5. This launches the agitated 'finale', culminating in T_4's orchestral conclusion and the third peak of intensity, in bar 688. Chopin's reversal of the usual tonal plan might have been prompted by his wish to close in the more 'tragic' E minor, rather than the comparatively bright parallel major that would more naturally have followed the second theme's recapitulatory statement in that key. In any case, by employing this scheme he transfers structural weight towards the end,[30] although the first episode's powerful progression to V corresponds in expressive effect to a typical sonata-form modulation towards the second theme.

bar:	1	61	139	179	222	283	333	385	474	486	510	534	573	605	621	671–89
thematic group/section:	1, 2		1 episode 1		2 episode 2		( )	development		1 episode 3 (≈episode 1)			2	*	'finale'	coda
tutti/solo:	T_1		S_1				T_2	S_2		T_3	S_3					T_4
main key:	i (E minor)				→v I (E major)			VI ---→ V		i (E minor)			III (→v) i (G major) (E minor)		i (E minor)	i
hypothetical key scheme:	i (E minor)				III (G major)			VI ---→ V		i (E minor)			I (E major)		I (E major) i or I? (E minor? E major?)	i or I?
dynamic peaks:					fff bar 210			fff bar 478								fff† bar 688

*expressive goal

† in Chopin's piano reduction

Figure 4.5 Op. 11, i: form and tonal plan

Narrative

The first tutti (at $\quartnote = 126$, much faster than the sluggish tempos in most recordings) generates terrific energy from the start, due to the registrally expansive theme 1a in the upper parts and 'lamentational' chromatic descent in the lower strings, bassoon and trombone. Noteworthy thematic features include angular dotted rhythms, implied hemiolas and the melodic shape in bar 7 (virtually identical to an idea in Hummel's Op. 85), its C to B motion ($\hat{6} \to \hat{5}$) to assume motivic importance throughout the concerto. The opening eight-bar phrase – a balanced 4 + 4, as at the start of Op. 21 – returns in the subdominant in bar 9, only to be interrupted by a *forzato* diminished chord four bars later. Here a quiet dialogue within winds and strings precedes another violent tutti outburst at *ff*, these jarring contrasts acting as a leitmotif in what follows. After repeating this passage and reaching a more definitive climax in bars 20–3, Chopin moves to the 'main theme', 1b, presented without the exquisite ornamentation to come in S_1.[31] Accompanied by fragments of theme 1a, the continuation from bar 33 differs from the later piano version, bar 45's forceful dominant preceding a more emollient transition to the second theme.

Played initially by the strings, with horn, flute and bassoon added afterward, theme 2 is cantabile and legato, offering a hiatus from the abrupt contrasts thus far. Within four successive phrases (a, a', b, a''), Chopin's archetypal phraseology prevails – namely, an ascending motion balanced by an often extended descent. The progressively richer instrumental palette, particularly when the theme returns in a'' (doubled in octaves, as was the intervening melody in b), raises the temperature, until bar 91's interruption releases energy towards bar 99 – analogous to bars 45ff. but in C major, which eventually resolves to the dominant in a harmonic version (VI $\to$ V) of the $\hat{6} \to \hat{5}$ melodic motion discussed earlier. Within this twice-stated climactic passage, Chopin again swings between *ff* and *p*, these oppositions making the coda in bars 123–38 seem especially subdued.

The soloist's *fortissimo* outburst articulates a fragment of theme 1a in double octaves followed by an energetic right-hand sweep[32] from the E below middle C up to e^4, answered by a twisting descent in sixths leading to V of A minor. In bar 147 the octave material returns in the sub-

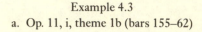

Example 4.3
a. Op. 11, i, theme 1b (bars 155–62)

dominant (compare T_1), heading after more semiquaver convolutions towards the E minor cadence closing the *Eingang*.[33] After a brief cello link, the piano intones theme 1b in a passage of overwhelming intensity (see Example 4.3a). The left hand's throbbing rhythms drive the yearning melody (more rhythmically insistent and vocally conceived than in T_1), while the glissando-like *fioriture* in bars 161, 164, 165 and 177 contrast with the plainer shapes around them, effortlessly transporting the hands between registers. The plasticity of line is remarkable (compare Kalkbrenner's superficially similar melody – Example 4.3b), likewise Chopin's manipulation of register, rhythm and melody,[34] which contains a rich array of figurations, all carefully judged. When the opening paragraph draws to a close after climaxing in bar 175, it is as if a profound transformation has occurred in just twenty bars, its impact to be felt throughout the movement.

Appropriately, the ensuing episode in bars 179ff. is initially reticent, quite unlike the boisterous *Spielepisoden* of Chopin's contemporaries. Innovative contrapuntal textures predominate (as in theme 1b) rather than bravura passagework, the offbeat tenor countermelodies for instance shadowing an upper-line melody, itself prepared by zigzag patterns rich in voice-leading implications. The figuration emerges naturally under the fingers and grows difficult only later (although remaining pianistic), having meanwhile explored various registers and keys over an

Example 4.3
b. Kalkbrenner, Op. 61, i, bars 105–12

ostinato-like left hand, whose regularity prepares the branching-out from bar 193 onwards. At this point the texture becomes more homophonic, with paired chromatic descents and convoluted shapes at alternating loud and soft dynamic levels (yet more juxtaposed opposites). Bar 203's *con fuoco* interjection heightens tension, which builds over eight bars in an extended, instrumentally highlighted voice exchange between A♯ and C towards bar 210's *fff* peak and the dominant's arrival in bar 211, whereupon parallel diminished sevenths chromatically slide to the more stable dominant prolongation in bars 215–21. Another voice exchange then guides further convolutions as the episode reaches its climax, with a winding-down passage to follow before theme 2's entrance in bar 222. Although the key itself does not change in episode 1, it achieves the sense of departure from the exposition's first group characteristic of sonata forms. The passage's emotional logic is faultless, Chopin's control of momentum masterful.[35]

The second theme – which resembles theme 1b in outline (see Example 4.4) – is comparatively calm and simple, accompanied by captivating tenor countermelodies recalling those in the preceding episode, although here they occasionally double the soprano part. As before, a ternary construction is utilised (that is, a, a′, b, a″), with a repeat of the opening eight-bar phrase after an 'interlude' in the dominant. In a′, the melody is accompanied by a horn obbligato; in b, octave doublings again

Example 4.4 Thematic isomorphism in Op. 11, i

feature,[36] as in the registrally more expansive a″ (bars 246ff.), which culminates in an emotionally intense passage akin to theme 2's recitative-like conclusion in the Maestoso of Op. 21. Although in Op. 11 Chopin reserves his most impassioned outpouring for the recapitulation, the music nevertheless becomes tortured and introspective, the successive 7–6 suspensions and disguised circle-of-fifths sequence in bars 259ff. enhancing its poignancy, likewise the long appoggiaturas in bars 255 and 257 (to be played on the beat, according to a liaison in Dubois), the sighing figures in bars 272–4 and the subtle wind colours in bars 266–72. The second theme's serenity quickly evaporates, the sombre mood of the opening continually threatening to return.

But in bar 275 E major's sudden arrival (initially in second inversion) dispels these shadows,[37] and Chopin deftly opens out the music towards the *risoluto* episode starting in bar 283. A celebratory spirit prevails as the highly original figuration grows more excited, although a *delicatissimo* touch is continually required, even in the soaring, *ben marcato* arpeggios through the circle of fifths in bars 291–4, later restated in bars 307–10. Episode 2 as a whole is simple in design. Bars 283–98 are repeated in bars 299–314, followed by an increasingly frenetic extension towards the breathtaking dissonances of bars 322–8, created by parallel diminished harmonies over a dominant pedal – once again, a clouding of harmony before structural clarification, in this case the start of T_2 in bar 333. Throughout the episode, Chopin employs his standard 'finale' technique: that is, concatenating short units of material suddenly extended to build momentum. Release comes only with the orchestral explosion at *ff* in bar 333, after the requisite trill (as in Op. 21, framed by tremolos) and last-minute left-hand enunciations of theme 1a's head motive within the dominant-seventh harmony.

The tutti's diminished-seventh interruption provokes impassioned playing like that in bars 45ff. and 99ff., this time exploiting earlier hemiola implications while developing theme 1a. After a sequential elaboration of the opening motive punctuated by *forzato* chords and ascending chromatically in the treble, from $f\sharp^2$ to b^2, the metre shifts one beat in bar 349, propelling the music through a counterbalancing descending sequence which stops dead with the exposed horn octaves on E in bars 355–6, played at an arresting p. Here returns the suspensive dialogue from bars 13ff. (now between upper and lower winds), rather like a voice from the past effecting the kind of 'time travel' necessary for structural integration in music. This is followed by a brief tutti swell to an energetic restatement of bars 39–40 in the tonic, a varied repeat of which gives way to further development thereof – yet more evidence of Chopin's 'organic' technique. The winding-down passage from bar 369 onwards proceeds somewhat deliberately towards S_2, which begins after a hushed coda analogous to that before S_1, although the key now changes to C major (VI).

The soloist's *dolce ed espressivo* restatement of theme 1b in the new key is all the more glorious for its relative simplicity, the pulsating left-hand chords supporting a melody shorn of ornamentation. Only in bar 391 is there a stylised sighing figure, marked 'leggierissimo'.[38] Almost immediately, however, the music turns to A minor (bar 393), prompting a recitative-inspired effusion like that in Op. 21 at precisely the same point. The melodic figuration grows agitated, especially in bars 397–8, where the right hand tortuously descends, with even more plaintive shapes to follow. All of this is supported by another 'lamentational' bass progression, from A (bar 393) through G$\sharp$ (bar 395), G$\natural$ (bar 397) and F (bar 399) to the low E in bar 407, the start of the development proper.

Whereas Op. 21's corresponding section betrays structural weaknesses, Op. 11's development is potent and expertly constructed, with four principal sections: bars 408–31, which start in V of iv (compare Op. 21);[39] a transposed, partial restatement in bars 432–47 (beginning in V); a large-scale 'crescendo' in bars 448–73; and the retransition in bars 474–85, which builds tension over a dominant pedal. The figuration is highly inventive, comprising some eight different types (among them, parallel first-inversion chords; arpeggiations, both unembellished and decorated by 'reaching-over' shapes; scales; *Rollfiguren*) and unfolding alongside developmental statements of theme 1a in the orchestra and, more dramatically, in the piano (bars 466–9). Typically these patterns are disposed over two- or four-bar periods in the up–down shape identified earlier, but occasionally Chopin changes contour to fuel momentum, as in bars 448ff. (down–up), 450 and 454 (contrary motion), and 474–85, where an extended arch spans some twelve bars, catapulting the music onto T_3's downbeat in bar 486. Harmonically the section is discursive but stable, with sequential activity connecting four closely related 'pillars': E major (bar 408), B major (424), F♯ major (448) and, eventually, B major, as V (474). The various sequences include descents by step (bars 448–56), by thirds (bars 456–62) and by fourths (bars 462–70), as well as ascents by step (bars 416–22 and 440–6). After the bold enharmonic shift from B♯^{o7} to C major in bars 470–1, the magnificent S_2 closes with a dramatic swell to the second peak of intensity – *fff*, bar 478 – after which the orchestral recapitulation of theme 1a provides much-needed catharsis.

Only the first twenty-four bars return, however,[40] and the piano enters in bar 510 not with theme 1a's 'announcement' but with theme 1b, which sounds vulnerable divested of its extrovert introduction. Its different effect on second hearing is further caused by variants in articulation, rhythm and figuration (often ignored by performers and editors). Small but significant alterations also affect the following episode (compare for instance bars 197–202 and 552–7), although bar 558's new direction is more profound in impact, eliding bars 203–10 and effecting a modulation towards G major (III), which arrives after a varied transposition of bars 211–21.

The second theme also sounds fresh and new, in part because of its different harmonic context but principally due to rhythmic and registral changes (note also the bassoon's obbligato in bars 581–8). Separating the two hands, Chopin now elaborates the tenor countermelody, its repeated offbeat rhythm (♪ ♩ ♩) more insistently shadowing the soprano line. Once again he uses different slurrings, fragmenting the melody in quasi-improvisatory fashion for greater vehemence (for instance, in b's first four bars, three slurs replace one), although the mood remains *dolce con espressione* at least until bar 600's change of direction. The phrase extension here briefly restores E minor (bar 604) before an emotional release even more impassioned than that in bars 397ff. ('stretto', 'sempre stretto'). As at the corresponding moment in Hummel's Op. 85 (which might have inspired this passage), the right hand 'improvises' a vocal melody – complete with *fioriture*, turns, glissandos and the *cercar della nota* appoggiaturas discussed in Chapter 2 – over a chord-outlining left hand which, in steady quavers, allows the treble to move with rhythmic freedom, in keeping with Chopin's *bel canto*-derived rubato. This is the movement's emotional goal, building naturally from theme 1b and putting everything into perspective, the sense of inexorability achieved partly by the slow, conjunct bass motion in dotted minims, and partly by the containment of the vocal figuration above, which, despite its efforts, never manages to break free.

Whereas the typical 'brilliant' concerto would launch into a last burst of keyboard virtuosity hereafter, Chopin relates his 'finale' to what came before, especially episodes 1 and 3 (compare their phrase structure, rhythm, figuration and harmonic outline) as well as theme 1b – a compatibility exploited by Balakirev (see p. 37). It also grows naturally from the anguish moments earlier. A three-part texture initially prevails, the middle-voice melody in quavers accompanied by semiquavers above and a left-hand ostinato uncannily like bars 24–35 of Moscheles' Op. 58, second movement, although used differently. The orchestra also employs ostinato patterns to ground the music before the dramatic branching-out that follows B minor's establishment in bar 637 (where the material from bars 621–6 returns transposed), with the tonic re-entering in bar 645. Chopin's 'finale' technique is used thereafter, short units being repeated, then extended, to build momentum towards the radical sequence initiated in bar 653 (the restored E♭s in bar 658 of Stirling making it even bolder). Here too phrase rhythm is effectively manipulated (bars 653–60 break down to 2, 2, 1, 1, 1 + 1 bars), and when the second-inversion dominant arrives in bar 661 tensions could hardly be greater. But the immediate retraction to *p* further electrifies the music, likewise the acciaccatura shapes articulated first by the right hand and then the left, until the chromatic slide in bars 665–6 surges to the tremolando trills over the next four bars, accompanied by theme 1a's main motive in the left hand. The interrupted cadence on C major comes as a shock, although the ensuing restatement of bars 111–22 (with some changes in instrumentation) makes good sense, as does the return of bars 131–4 afterwards. Nevertheless, the dynamic extremes in the closing

bar:	1	13	23	31	46	54	64	72	80	95	101	105	114–26
theme/ section:	introduction	a	b_1	b_2	codetta	a'	c	b_1'	b_2'	codetta'	'cadenza'	a''	coda
main key:		I	V - - - V			I	vi $\rightarrow$ $V/_{vi}$ $\approx$ iii		III♯			I	I

Figure 4.6 Op. 11, ii: form and tonal plan

bars – from *p* in bars 676–87 to *ff* (or *fff*) in bars 688–9 – jar somewhat, reminding us of one of the principal dramatic devices used throughout the movement.

Indeed, this discussion has revealed an all-embracing expressive plan with four main elements: a principle of contrast partly defined by stark dynamic juxtapositions within the orchestral accompaniment, working in combination with graded dynamic changes towards various climax points; a symbiotic relationship between themes and 'passagework', evident for instance in the melodic character of the episodic material; a sound, if idiosyncratic, key scheme whereby the retention of the tonic for the second theme in the exposition is 'allowed' by the strength of the climax in the preceding episode, and necessitated by the desired return to the tonic minor for the 'finale'; and the critical role of the recitative-like passages at the end of both statements of theme 2, the latter of which astounds by its intensity in preparing for the highly charged conclusion. This expressive plan – which takes one step further the compositional process underlying Op. 21's first movement – offers a strategy for performing the music in an original creative spirit, and thus for achieving the masterpiece in sound so ecstatically proclaimed by Lenz.

Op. 11, Romance

Form and tonal plan

The second movement – another finely wrought 'tone poem' – is no less singular than the first. Like Op. 21's Larghetto, the Romance draws upon Chopin's nocturne style, with a right-hand cantilena 'sung' over a gently undulating left-hand accompaniment. The movement also features the nocturne's typically ternary construction, although, as Figure 4.6 shows, its formal scheme is more complex than that of most nocturnes. After an orchestral introduction, the piano enters with theme a, which remains within the tonic area. This leads to a second thematic complex (b_1, b_2) in V, followed by a two-part codetta. At first, a's return in bar 54 has closural properties, like the third part of a ternary form, but the music branches out at bar 64 with a new *agitato* section, c, initially in C♯ minor (vi), its dominant reached in bar 71. Here a simple shift to G♯ minor marks the developmental return of b_1 in the movement's emotional climax, and when b_2 re-enters in bar 80 in G♯ major, its effect is consolatory. After the transposed codetta (in III♯) and a brief 'cadenza', theme a makes its final appearance, and with the tonic firmly re-established, a two-part coda concludes the Romance. Its central harmonic 'pillars' – I, III♯ and I, related by a major third – are thus linked by a I–V–I motion in the first half and a progression through C♯ minor in the second, this tonal plan operating in tandem with the three statements of theme a that constitute the movement's formal bedrock.

Narrative

Parallels between Chopin's Romance and the slow movements of his principal models are manifold. Most open with an orchestral introduction, followed by the piano's initial, nocturne-like appearance without orchestra; modulation to the dominant typically occurs after this first theme in a large-scale ternary design capped by a two-part coda. Here the similarities end, however, for Chopin's slow movement flows far more effortlessly and integrally than any other, transcending the melodic constipation of Field's A♭ major Concerto and the gratuitous virtuosity of Kalkbrenner Op. 61 and Hummel Opp. 85 and 89. Even his introduction is 'organically' conceived, comprising four statements of an ascending melody in dialogue between muted first violins and cellos, and articulating the principal structural harmonies to follow: E major (I), B major (V), C♯ minor (vi) and G♯ major (V of vi). The two cello ascents also reappear later, likewise bar 2's C♯ → B ($\hat{6}$ → $\hat{5}$) motion.

After the Allegro maestoso's intensity, the quiet and restrained opening (at ♩ = 80) comes as a relief, as does the utterly simple piano solo that follows. Marked 'cantabile' (see Example 4.5), it demonstrates Chopin's increasing ability to generate momentum from within the musical line, in this case through successive attempts to achieve melodic closure. Bars 13–14 and bars 15–16 both move from g♯² to f♯², stopping on the dominant harmony; a third melodic phase in bar 17 then proceeds from g♯² to a² (implied in bar 18 and stated in bar 19), the ensuing motion from f♯² to e² interrupted by bar 20's inflection to C♯ minor; and not until bar 22 is e² definitively reached, at the end of the last, four-bar melodic segment.[41] Chopin fills in this 'dynamic' outline with subtly varied

Example 4.5 Op. 11, ii, bars 13–15[1] and 54–6[1]

rhythms and figurations, the stylised *portamento* in bar 17 expanding registrally to a brief climax before a final winding-down to bar 22's cadence in I.

Although concise, the orchestral link to b_1 deftly moves to B major (V), effected by antiphonal statements of a tonicising linear motion G♯–A♯–B in first and second violins. The piano then blossoms with a gorgeous melody, intoned over a contrapuntally rich nocturne accompaniment (see Example 4.6). Here and throughout, variation infuses the music, Chopin's innovative, elastic figuration masking the underlying similarity of bars 23 and 25. As the melody soars from $f\sharp^2$, the rhythm initially growing faster (shaped by the 'accelerando principle') but then restrained, one expects it to continue to e^3, the tenor's fourth-quaver e^1 in bar 24 delicately reinforcing this anticipation underneath the sustained dissonance. But in the event, the soprano falls a major seventh, thus inspiring the more passionate figuration in the next bar, itself answered by the sighing *strascino* (that is, inverted *portamento*) connecting $c\sharp^3$ to $d\sharp^2$. Without drawing a breath, the melody begins a crescendo through sequential harmonies and higher registers while indulging in incessantly varied figuration (compare beats 1–2 and 3–4 in bars 27 and 28). The climax reached in bars 29–30 is a graded one, however, for Chopin immediately retracts to **pp** with the *dolcissimo*

Example 4.6 Op. 11, ii, bars 23–6 and 72–5

cadence on V that leaves b_1 open for the more extended b_2 to follow. One's only regret is that this glorious passage lasts but eight bars.

The new section is periodic in construction – a pair of phrases (first eight, then seven bars) made up of two two-bar ideas answered by a cadential progression over several bars. As before, however, the sheer wealth of figuration obscures this outline to the point that bars 39–42 sound like new material rather than an embellished version of bars 31–4. Although simple at first, the music soon grows effusive in the increasingly elaborate melodic arches, especially at the apex of the four-bar extension in bars 35–8. Bar 39's more conjunct treble moves in thirds with doubly rich chromaticism filling the gaps of the arpeggio outline from before (crucial misprints being corrected in Stirling's score). In both of the 'answering' bars (40 and 42), Chopin's slurring works against the beat, effecting an impetus that eventually inspires a broader, climactic progression to the cadence on V in bars 43–5. The codetta, in two parts, winds down by repeating its initial two-bar idea – with more variation the second time, including an exquisite *fioritura* in bar 49, 'diminuendo e rallentando' – and then progressively liquidating a final closing pattern from two beats to one, until bar 52's brief silence. Here the muted upper strings proceed towards the reprise, while the cello restates a rhythmically varied form of its first melodic ascent in the introduction.

A' thus seems a point of return, its richer ornamentation generating structural weight, as Example 4.5 suggests, even though a refinement of detail prevails, as for instance in the breathtaking *fioriture* of bars 54 and 58 and the variants entered in Stirling's and Hartmann's copies (see p. 114). The return at bar 60 to the opening's simpler outlines assumes prominence, as do the telling C♮s in bar 61 that fleetingly suggest a darker mood. Indeed, after the portentous bassoon and horn announcement of bar 63, idyllic lyricism gives way to anguish and agitation. Within the new key of C♯ minor (vi), the left hand's polyphony and the orchestra's nagging ostinato support a new right-hand melody registrally discursive and ingeniously varied in rhythm, an outpouring of no less intensity than the recitative in Op. 21's Larghetto (not to mention the recitative-inspired passages in the first movements of both concertos). Shaped with Chopin's *bel canto* rubato, the vocally conceived line hints at b_1 in bar 68 (compare bar 23) before drawing breath on V of C♯ minor in bar 71, the left hand shadowed by the double bass's G♯–F$_x$ murmur. The right hand then changes to octaves as if to intone its 'sotto voce' expressive message in two parts, while the left hand embarks on another 'lamentational' bass descent, moving chromatically from G♯ to D♯. Both the resultant 5–6 sequence and the passage's different ambience disguise its kinship with b_1 (see Example 4.6), the initial two-bar idea stated twice before a four-bar arch shape achieves the movement's expressive peak and an 'open' cadence on V of G♯ minor.

When b_2 re-enters in G♯ major in bar 80, it exudes a sense of rediscovery after a brief but difficult emotional journey. Nevertheless, there is much new, not only the key but also the figuration, dynamics, slurring and other articulation. For instance, the huge, *leggierissimo* leaps in bar 91 provide impetus to the repeated passage, likewise the more ambitious run ('forte e veloce') in bars 93–4 and, within the codetta, the gnarled *fioritura* in bar 98, after which the second part of the codetta returns verbatim. Once again clouding the harmony before a structural resolution, Chopin indulges in breathtaking parallel diminished harmonies within a 'cadenza' that, underneath the surface colours, prolongs G♯ major.[42] From there the music proceeds to the tonic for a's final statement, prepared by the cello's ascent from bar 8 – yet another use of the introductory material, effecting large-scale connection.

Theme a is played by the strings while the piano engages in gossamer

bar:	1	17	100	120	168	212	280	328	340	412	456–520
section:	introduction	A	orch'l link	episode 1	B	episode 2	* A'	orch'l link	episode 3	B'	'finale'
theme:		theme 1 (a a b a' interlude a'')			theme 2		theme 1 (a' interlude a''')			theme 2	
main key:	$V/_{vi}$→V→I I (E major)			vi→$V/_{IV}$	IV (A major)	→V	I (E major)		III♯→$V/_V$ V (B major)		I (E major)

*false reprise in E♭ major

Figure 4.7 Op. 11, iii: form and tonal plan

figuration of considerable colouristic variety while deftly exploiting cross-accentual rhythmic implications (especially in bar 110). But after this last thematic utterance, the rhythm grows more regular in the coda, which, like the codettas, has two parts. The first comprises two asymmetrical phrases, bars 114–18 and 119–22, both of which engage the piano in down–up arpeggio patterns accompanied by strings, horn and bassoon, with other winds added later to almost Mendelssohnian effect. The mood is peaceful, even when the harmony briefly darkens in bar 122 (note the telling C♮s, as in bar 61), after which the focus remains fixed on the tonic, bar 125's last-minute intonations of the $\hat{6} \rightarrow \hat{5}$ motive recalling others moments before (bars 118 and 122) as well as earlier in the movement. As the music winds down, 'the half-tints of an evening twilight dissolve harmoniously' at the end of a Romance whose ingenious invention and effortless flow define a compositional style that would shape much of Chopin's music for almost two decades to come.

Op. 11, Rondo

Form and tonal plan

Unlike Op. 21's Allegro vivace, this movement is expressly designated 'Rondo'; it is also in the tonic major rather than minor – an important difference possibly attributable to its dance model, the krakowiak. Two of Chopin's independent rondos – Op. 5 (*Rondo à la mazur*) and Op. 16 – follow the tonal scheme used here: I–IV–I–V–I, corresponding to the principal thematic sections, A–B–A'–B'–'finale'.[43] In all three pieces, lengthy episodes join the thematic 'pillars', the main difference being Chopin's integration of the successive formal units here, as opposed to the concatenated sprawl of the other rondos.[44] As Figure 4.7 indicates, the movement starts with an orchestral introduction (marked 'Vivace ♩ = 104'). This prepares the first theme's appearance in section A, which itself is in rondo form, comprising three versions of the theme (a, a', a'') interspersed with contrasting material (b, which develops theme 1, and an orchestral interlude). A concluding passage links section A to the first episode, which immediately moves from the tonic to C♯ minor (vi) and then embarks on a modulatory course to IV. Here section B begins, its short orchestral introduction preparing theme 2. An even more discursive episode proceeds to the dominant, whereupon section A' and theme 1 commence, preceded by a false reprise in E♭ major. Only section A's latter half returns, however, and a similar abbreviation deflects the ensuing orchestral transition towards G♯ major (III♯, initially as V of vi – compare the introduction) and the start of episode 3, the longest and most elaborate of all. Having built terrific momentum, Chopin reaches the dominant for section B's second statement, which restores the tonic in anticipation of the 'finale', its spellbinding virtuosity completing a cumulative process that spans the four episodes and accrues energy throughout the movement.

Narrative

Just as the mazurka influenced Op. 21's Allegro vivace,[45] this movement derives both small-scale features and an overall control of impulse and shape from the krakowiak. For instance, the orchestral opening and theme 1 use a characteristic rhythm: [♫ ♩] (x_1), reinterpreted afterward as [♫ ♪] (x_2) and [♫ | ♪] (y_1), the latter giving rise to [♪ | ♪] (y_2). Another ubiquitous cell – [♬♬ ♪] (z) – also stems from the krakowiak, a lively folkdance in 2/4 (versus the mazurka's triple metre). The *risoluto* opening uses two statement–response patterns between strings and winds, alternating between *ff* and *pp* over eight bars, followed by an initially syncopated consequent that gradually dwindles to pizzicato fifths in the lower strings just before the piano enters. The latter's *scherzando* theme, first played without orchestral accompaniment, unfolds at *p* over an oscillating left hand as in Op. 14, with snapped rhythms, trills, turns, grace notes (played on the beat, as shown in Dubois) and Lydian fourths adding brilliance. After reaching the dominant (compare bar 17 of the *Rondo à la krakowiak*), the eight-bar phrase is repeated with orchestra, followed by a developmental passage (b) initially in the supertonic minor, again as in Op. 14. Here, however, Chopin lengthily prolongs the dominant harmony that follows, the skipping figuration in bars 44–5 answered by flutes and clarinets just before the first of the descending sequences used 'motivically' at several cadence points. When the *scherzando* theme returns, it proceeds differently, rising sequentially through ii and IV to V and then to the tonic, a second sequential descent ending this section.

Obliquely derived from theme 1, the ensuing interlude capitalises on the music's earlier buoyancy, paring away ornamentation and bombastically presenting various rhythmic cells in bare outline. For instance, the horn octaves in bars 77–80 articulate z and x_1 in successive p–$f\!f$ pairs that generate momentum towards bar 86's dominant climax, the goal of a I–iii–V progression initiated in bar 72. But an immediate retraction occurs with the returning cadential sequence from bars 48ff., used to launch a final, varied restatement of theme 1 (a″) noteworthy for the acciaccatura-like leaps in its consequent and the added horn pedal on b^1. The theme now has strong closural properties, as does the orchestral passage that concludes the first section, articulating motives from theme 1 (for example, in bars 104 *et seq.*) and rhythmic cells such as x_1 and z (intermeshed in bars 100ff.). As earlier, Chopin makes expert use of the orchestra, contrapuntally combining different instrumental timbres while inventively employing rhythmic devices like those above. It is hard to imagine this colourful passage in the solo–piano format that Chopin himself might have used on occasion.

After a powerful cadence exploiting a syncopated rhythm typical of the krakowiak (♪♩♪), the piano returns with its first explicitly loud dynamic – '$f\!f$ risoluto' – in the first of the three episodes, which starts with announcement material in C♯ minor analogous to that in Op. 21's third movement and in Op. 22. Here it comprises a chord, then an arpeggio sweep, arranged in dialogue with strings, then winds. The passage-work that follows introduces a pattern maintained almost constantly hereafter, in which a left-hand quaver pulse punctuates right-hand triplet–semiquaver figurations. The first is a stylised snap, effortlessly articulated under the fingers thanks to its keyboard disposition. Chopin states the one-bar idea twice, provides a lilting two-bar response, repeats these four bars and then transposes the whole passage to B major (V) over sixteen bars. At bar 144, however, a broader gesture sets in, supported by a circle-of-fifths sequence in the bass interrupted by bar 148's A major. Short units again prevail, followed by more expansive gestures, bars 152–5 impelling the music onto bar 156's downbeat, whereupon Chopin reinforces the newly established V of A major with a repeated, two-bar sequential idea and then another 'motivic' cadential descent (compare bars 160–7 with bars 48–51 and 64–7). Its goal is the subdominant harmony with which section B begins in bar 168.

In their brief introduction, the upper strings play 'pp e leggiero' over a zigzagging pizzicato cello, rhythm z serving as an ostinato here and virtually throughout the section. Even the second theme uses it, although differently positioned within the bar. Disposed in octaves (like its counterpart in Op. 21 – see p. 59), the new theme contains another manifestation of the $\hat{6} \rightarrow \hat{5}$ motive permeating the previous movements. Both the melodic outline and its harmonic support are skeletal, save for a few on-the-beat ornaments providing colour. One reason for this 'economy' is to allow variations in the recapitulation to assume prominence – a tactic repeatedly used in the first and second movements, as shown earlier. But Chopin also effects thereby a hushed if lighthearted mood, energised by the chugging strings and pizzicato cello. Basically section B amounts to four thematic statements: in A major (IV), B minor (ii of IV), F major ($\natural$VI of IV) and, after a developmental extension, A major. The temperature then rises with syncopations (rhythm y_2) and a crescendo to bar 208's $f\!f$, whereupon a fourth cadential sequence descends in the piano, answered by orchestral punctuation.

Episode 2 starts playfully, the opening right-hand melody exploiting the $\hat{6} \rightarrow \hat{5}$ motive with rhythm y_2 below. Not until bar 220 do triplet semiquavers penetrate the treble, having previously been in the left hand (which later states the evocative rhythm x_1 in bars 221 and 225). At this point the passagework commences in earnest, moving over eight bars from I through iii to V in A major, the last of these being reinforced in a descending chromatic sequence towards the more expansive section from bar 232. Although the figuration then changes, Chopin continues to use melodic ideas[46] and rhythms from before, among them ♩ ♪♪ | ♩ (compare bars 220–1 and 223–4 *et seq.* with bars 233–4ff.), these links creating cohesion rather as mazurka-inspired variation does in Op. 21's third movement. Over twelve bars (232–44^1), the bass foundation linearly ascends through a fifth, supporting short units characteristically followed by broader gestures. Once the dominant is reached, Chopin retracts to p (despite the explicitly *brillante* figuration); but with the scales in sixths in bars 248–9 and snapping figures in bars 251–2, energy again rises. The section's harmonic goal having been attained, what follows serves to delay the reprise by means of highly original figuration, an expertly judged phrase structure, and subtle deployment of register and dynamics. When the retransition proper begins in bar 264, section A's return seems inevitable – hence the listener's surprise at the false recapitulation of theme 1 in E♭ major in bar 272.[47] Marked 'a tempo' (although most performers take it slower), this gentle but teasing section lasts only eight bars – the first four in a weak second-inversion 'tonic' – after which Chopin enharmonically slides to E major's dominant for the full-blown reprise.

Section A' imitates its predecessor until the fifth and last statement of theme 1, a''', where Chopin adds an insistent inverted pedal on B (note especially rhythm x_2), underneath which the inner fingers of the right hand trace a twisting variant particularly chromatic in bar 323. Like a'', this passage has a closural feel (partly due to the framing E–B fifth), likewise the tutti from bar 100 that re-enters only to be diverted at bar 332 by a developmental version of its continuation plangently intoned by clarinets, bassoons and horns. Moving directly to C♯ minor, the orchestral link is abbreviated by eight bars, its final cadential 'echo' elided by bar 337's rush towards the third episode, which commences vigorously in V of C♯ minor.

This lengthy passage combines numerous figurations in short or extended phrases over a simple bass motion from G♯ through F♯ (bar 364) to E (bar 372) and then via E♯ (bar 388) to F♯ (bar 392), whereupon a massive build-up to the dominant and theme 2's return commences. The passage's brilliance is unparalleled in Chopin's early music, likewise its registral manipulation, rhythmic variety and balancing between stable phases and those threatening to disintegrate. For the first sixteen bars, the music stays tied to the G♯ pedal, the progressively shorter bass ideas towards the end supporting a huge arpeggio preparing for the up–down arch patterns that set in from bar 356. Over a steadily descending bass, these arpeggios[48] – which themselves alternate between long and short units – push towards bar 372's E, which instigates a new phase in the episode. Here the extremely rapid harmonic rhythm, taxing figuration and stark dynamic juxtapositions destabilise the music, as do the lightning registral shifts between the hands. Chopin's *con fuoco* reversal of the up–down pattern in bars 380ff., accompanied by left-hand allusions to theme 1 and rhythms x_1 and y_1, provokes even greater turbulence, and it is not until the diminished-seventh harmony on E♯ in bars 388ff. that stability returns, thanks to the restoration of regular up–down right-hand arpeggios and the punctuating x_1 below. The retransition that follows also settles the music with its graded increase in momentum above a dominant pedal (i.e. V of V). Over incessant articulations of x_1, Chopin twice repeats a registrally confined right-hand shape in four-bar units, branching out within the third statement to a dynamic and registral peak at bar 408 fuelled by the rhythmic acceleration below. The cascading arpeggio in bars 408–9 and the ascending scales that answer it arrive forcefully on section B's return in bar 412, setting the seal on a whirlwind episode that takes the movement to an even higher energy plane than in episodes 1 and 2.

Subtly varied in each successive statement, theme 2 follows its earlier course apart from a change of direction within the *dolcissimo* third phase, in G major (♮VI of V). Here the music heads not to B major, in which the section began, but to the tonic E major (the only *forte* iteration of theme 2 in the Rondo). It is in this key that the 'finale' starts in bar 456, this concluding section celebrating the tonic's definitive return by gradually attaining the highest energy level in the movement, to be generated over the next sixty-five bars. Arranged in groups of $1 + 1 + 2$ bars oscillating between tonic and dominant, the first sixteen bars feature 'snaps' in contrary motion based on rhythm x_1, a variant of y_1 and the $\hat{6} \rightarrow \hat{5}$ melodic pattern, answered by energetic up–down shapes. The more plaintive ascending sequence that follows (E–F♯–G♯–A, rising through A♯ to B) provides a brief hiatus before the rollicking sequential descent in fourths in bars 480–3 (E–B, D♮–A, C♮–B), repeated at f in the next four bars. Having splintered the line, Chopin now extends it with two four-bar up-and-down scales that lower the register for the fifth phase (bars 496ff.), its parallel octaves recalling the figuration at the start of episode 3. But now chromaticism infiltrates both the ascending scales and the crabbed arpeggio shape that enters in bar 504, restated in the next bar and answered by a smooth linear ascent and descent over two bars. After a repeat of these four bars, the registral level is restored to that of bar 496 (the intervening passage having thus inscribed a massive up–down arc), whereupon the pianist launches into two sets of arpeggios (the second achieving the movement's loudest dynamic, ff) and an exciting scale through four octaves, accompanied by the orchestra's tonic arpeggio over eight bars. A few tutti chords bring the Rondo to a triumphant close.

Although this movement retains both the alternation between theme and display characteristic of the *stile brillante* and the 'episodic' construction of Chopin's earlier rondos, it achieves an unprecedented degree of integration thanks to the composer's control of impulse and gesture, the 'passagework' possessing goal-directed qualities at both small and large levels within a series of ever-expanding trajectories. Like the other two movements, the Rondo 'adds up' to much more than the sum of its parts, its underlying structure and unfolding narrative united in expressive purpose – as in the finest performances of the work, among them no doubt Chopin's own.

Coda

Words can never fully capture musical experience: its temporal course and emotional impact ultimately lie beyond the powers of verbal description. This is particularly true of Chopin's concertos, which have suffered at the hands of writers unable (or unwilling) to respond to the music's time and sound dependency. The foregoing analytical re-evaluation is in one sense another futile attempt to encapsulate the concertos in words, but at least it has been undertaken in a spirit of appreciation, not denigration. If nothing else, it has revealed the utter hollowness of Niecks's criticisms and those of his successors, as summarised in Chapter 3 – specifically, concerning Chopin's poor control of form and tonal structure, the music's lack of development and organic unity, and the inept orchestration. On the basis of the analysis in this chapter, the first of these points can be dismissed out of hand: not only is there evidence of genius and inspiration within the structure of the two concertos, but it is equally clear that they work 'in time', in 'living sound' – and my commentary has taken pains to explain why, and how. As for lack of development, I have shown subtle connections that might have satisfied Niecks and others had they succeeded in discerning them (for instance, within the second thematic complex of Op. 21's Allegro vivace, or between theme b_1's two statements in the Romance), as well as a degree of coherence and compatibility at least implicitly sensed by Balakirev and others. Furthermore, the linking of the four episodes in Op. 11's Rondo in a single structural crescendo suggests a command of musical development far more significant than the 'organic unity' conferred by mere *thematische Arbeit*, likewise the 'emotional plan' in operation throughout the work's first movement – and indeed all the other movements. No apologies need be made for this music regarding its formal construction or integrity: in both respects, the two concertos can be regarded as unqualified masterpieces.

The matter of orchestration is less straightforward, however.[49] Throughout this re-evaluation I have alluded to the importance of the instrumental accompaniment, which I see as much more than just 'adequate', and certainly not the 'necessary but regrettable orchestral backgrounds' lamented by Abraham and 'improved' by the likes of Klindworth and Tausig. There are weaknesses to be sure. If only for practical reasons, Chopin heavily uses the strings to accompany solo passages, and he fails to achieve the consistent interplay between piano and orchestra so characteristic of Mozart and Beethoven. Registrally confined or otherwise conservative in design, the individual parts often lack flair – at least at the speeds taken in most performances. But one has only to listen to the superb results obtained by Abbado, Mehta and other conductors to realise that these orchestral accompaniments can be made to work in performance, and indeed to work well.

To play these concertos with orchestra is not a matter of making the best of a bad job: when 'vital' tempos are taken and over-rich sonorities avoided, the orchestral backdrop comes to life as a real partner to the soloist, without which much would be lost.[50] Particularly successful instances of cooperation between solo and orchestra include the ostinato effects in the 'finale' of Op. 11's first movement and the middle of the Romance, where the very consistency of the string parts throws the impassioned piano melody into relief. Another lies in the accompaniments to the second themes of both third movements, which, when kept rhythmically and metrically stable, ground the piano's flexible rubato above while timbrally enriching its melody in octaves. Other admirable features identified in my commentary include the wind and brass punctuation in Op. 21's first tutti; the dramatic recitative and piano–bassoon canon in the Larghetto; the arresting horn octaves and ensuing wind dialogue in the second tutti of Op. 11. There is of course much else to commend – far more, in fact, than there is to regret, provided that the soloist and conductor approach the music sympathetically, with a view to achieving the 'unusually profound effect' discerned by Merkel. It is possible to overcome any conceivable weaknesses simply by activating the expressive plans inscribed within this music, as Chopin himself did in the early 1830s and as the best performers continue to do over 160 years later.

Chopin's third concerto

Contexts

Chopin's enthusiasm for the *stile brillante* waned rapidly during his early years in Paris. Only a handful of virtuoso pieces follow the two concertos – among them, the *Grand duo concertant* for piano and cello on themes from Meyerbeer's *Robert le diable* (1831), the *Variations brillantes* Op. 12 on a theme of Hérold (1833) and the Rondo Op. 16 (ca 1833). None of these comes close to the concertos conceptually or expressively, and it is understandable why, having brought the *stile brillante* 'to perfection', Chopin should henceforth have favoured the more individual artistic style he had forged in Warsaw in the late 1820s and in Vienna and Paris from 1830 onwards. Nevertheless, his ongoing exploitation of virtuoso textures and procedures in other musical contexts remains one of his most significant compositional achievements. Starting with the Etudes Op. 10, Chopin utterly transformed the conventional gestures of the brilliant style, deriving new powers from the archetypal alternation between lyricism and display, and employing virtuosity for profoundly expressive purposes – as in the 'finales' of the four ballades, which employ a 'white heat of virtuosity' to 'exorcise earlier conflicts and tensions'.[1] These and other large-scale works – including the scherzos, fantasies and sonatas – indirectly draw upon the precedent set by Op. 11 and Op. 21, which themselves stand apart from the conventional by reinterpreting the traditions that shaped them.

Against this background, Chopin's *Allegro de concert*, published in 1841, comes as a surprise in its blatant exploitation of the *stile brillante*, only partially mediated by the stylistic consolidation of the 1830s. Possibly his most difficult piece, it belongs to a loosely defined genre embracing Bach's *Italian Concerto* (1735), Edward Wolff's *Grand allegro de concert* Op. 39 (1840)[2] and Alkan's 'Concerto' movements for solo piano within the *Douze Etudes* Op. 39 (1857),[3] in which the tutti–solo contrasts of the concerto were stylised in a piece for solo keyboard. It also has parallels with the solo versions of concertos played by contemporary composer-pianists when orchestral forces were unavailable or unsuitable for performance. But these precedents alone do not explain the hard-core virtuosity in Op. 46, which is difficult to square with Chopin's study of Kastner's and Cherubini's counterpoint treatises at the time,[4] and with such pioneering works as the Polonaise Op. 44, an innovative hybrid of two genres, polonaise and mazurka; the Prelude Op. 45, harmonically adventurous and generically distinct from the Preludes Op. 28; the great C minor Nocturne Op. 48 No. 1; and the Fantasy Op. 49, although it, like the *Allegro de concert*, reflects the French operatic style that influenced Chopin from early on.

Creation

References in Chopin's correspondence to a 'third concerto' occur as early as 22 December 1830, in a letter from Vienna to his family in Warsaw: '[Tomasz] Nidecki comes and plays here every morning. When I write my Concerto for two pianos we shall give its first performance together; but first of all I must appear as a soloist.'[5] Plans for this duo concerto apparently were abandoned (it is never again mentioned), and not until mid 1834 does a 'third concerto' resurface in the correspondence, in a letter from Chopin's father Nicolas (jointly written with his sister Izabela): 'By the way, you did not let us know whether you have finished your third concerto. I confess I doubt whether you have, and I should not be sorry if you had not, for it demands too much mental tension.'[6] Some months later, on 11 April 1835, Nicolas commented: 'You still haven't mentioned whether you have finished your third concerto or whether you are publishing the first one [i.e. the F minor].'[7] At about the same time, independent references to Chopin's 'third concerto' appear in letters between Breitkopf & Härtel in Leipzig and their Paris representative, Heinrich Albert Probst, who wrote on 2 October 1834: 'Would you like to engrave Chopin's second and third concertos? Each would cost 800–1000 francs, possibly only 600', to which the publisher responded two weeks later: 'You speak of Chopin's Concertos

Nos. 2 and 3. We are willing to engrave one of them, if you can get it for 500–600 francs. You know both well and have the choice; I don't want both at once, the third at least not until winter.'[8] As Jeffrey Kallberg observes: 'That Probst boasted he could obtain the work in 1834 might belie the notion that the concerto was never completed; at the very least, it suggests that the composition had developed to a point beyond that previously thought.'[9] Chopin himself performed 'un magnifique concerto de piano' at a Schlesinger soirée on 16 February 1834, as noted in Chapter 2.[10] Whether this was the as yet unpublished F minor Concerto or the eventual *Allegro de concert* remains unclear, as indeed does the identity of the work(s) referred to by Nicolas Chopin, Probst and Härtel.

The common assumption among scholars has been that Chopin fashioned Op. 46 from the residue of either the unfinished concerto for two pianos (if it was even started) or, more likely, the 'third concerto' mentioned in the early 1830s correspondence and possibly performed at Schlesinger's – a provenance now corroborated by a hitherto unpublished letter from Chopin to Breitkopf & Härtel dating from September 1841, to be discussed below. As for stylistic evidence, this points to a grounding in the early 1830s, with various details indicative of later developments – among others, the 'athletic', Lisztian technique required of its performer. But the work's chronology, however problematic, is less perplexing than the motivation behind its publication in 1841. Why did Chopin sanction the release of this eclectic and, in some ways, retrogressive piece at a time of stylistic consolidation and reassessment? To answer this question requires consideration of three factors: the reminiscences of both the work's dedicatee, Friederike Müller, and Dr Aleksander Hoffmann, a close friend of Chopin's; the young composer-pianist's experience in performing the E minor Concerto; and Op. 46's effect in sound – as opposed, yet again, to its embodiment in the score.

One of Chopin's 'disciples affectionnées', the talented Müller (dubbed 'Mademoiselle opus quarante-six' by Liszt) studied with Chopin from October 1839 to Spring 1841. She reports that on parting, 'he presented me with the two manuscripts of his C♯ major [*sic*] and E major studies (dedicated to Liszt), and promised to write during his stay in the country a concert-piece and dedicate it to me'[11] – thus revealing one possible reason for the work's realisation as Op. 46, that is, as a response to his pupil's exceptional abilities. Chopin's own first reference to the *Allegro de concert* as such occurs in a letter from Paris to Breitkopf & Härtel in Leipzig written about the same time, on 4 May 1841, stating: 'As I have now several compositions intended for publication (including an *Allegro de concert*, a Fantasia etc.) I should like you to be good enough to discuss the sale of these new works.'[12] Another letter from Chopin to the Leipzig publisher, dated 10 September 1841 and only recently brought to the attention of Chopin scholars, makes crystal clear the connection between the *Allegro de concert* and Chopin's 'third concerto', for he offers for publication an '<u>Allegro maestoso</u> (du 3me Concerto) pour piano seul', at a price of 1000 francs.[13] The revelation of this important document explains Chopin's wording in a letter of 9 October 1841 from Nohant to Fontana in Paris: 'Mme Sand's son will be in Paris about the 16th and will bring the manuscript of my concerto [*manuskrypt Koncertu*]' – this reference to the eventual Op. 46 as a 'concerto' once again confirming its origins.[14] Nine days later, Chopin wrote to Fontana: '[Masset] couldn't possibly expect me to sell him twelve Studies or a Piano–Method for 300 francs. The same applies to the Allegro maestoso [i.e. Op. 46] which I am sending today – he can't have it for 300 – not less than 600.'[15]

Instructing Fontana again on 20 October 'to take care of my Allegro',[16] Chopin sent Breitkopf & Härtel autograph manuscripts of Opp. 46, 47, 48 and 49 on 12 November 1841.[17] The first of these served as a *Stichvorlage* for the German first edition of the *Allegro de concert*, published by Breitkopf in December 1841 (plate no. 6651), while a copy by Fontana was used in preparing Schlesinger's French first edition (plate no. 3481), released on 28 November 1841 with a second impression soon to follow. This corrected certain typographical errors and omissions but not the time signature,[18] which steadfastly remains C as opposed to the ¢ of the autograph, Fontana's copy and the other early editions – including Wessel's, which appeared in January 1842 (plate no. 5298).[19] Chopin's autograph and Fontana's copy survive; the latter (Morgan Library, New York) is generally faithful to the former (Biblioteka Narodowa, Warsaw), apart from some missing accidentals, dynamics and articulation marks, and occasional inaccuracies in transcribing grace notes. These appear to have been overlooked by Chopin himself, who added tempo, dynamic and pedal indications to the copy.

There is no known record of Chopin performing the *Allegro de concert* in public (apart, perhaps, from the Schlesinger soirée in 1834, in its earlier incarnation as part of the 'third concerto'). According to Marceli Antoni Szulc, he wished to reserve the finished work for a particularly significant occasion:

> Chopin himself held this piece in high regard. He played it in manuscript form to A. Hoffmann to gain his opinion, and after receiving the praise it naturally and appropriately deserved, he responded with these words: 'This is the very first piece I shall play in my first concert upon returning home to a free Warsaw.'[20]

Such a performance would of course never take place. Chopin did however hear Müller play the work in late 1844 or early 1845,[21] and glosses indicate that he taught it to Dubois – chief among them a cut from bar 12 to bar 82, possibly for (optional?) use in performance.[22] There are also handwritten emendations in the scores of Franchomme and Chopin's sister Ludwika Jędrzejewicz, the latter sometimes attributed to the composer.[23] The fingerings and other markings in Franchomme's copy are not in Chopin's hand, having probably been entered after his death in 1849, by which time Op. 46 had embarked on a journey through the critical world no smoother than that of Op. 11 or Op. 21.

Interpretation

Writers have not on the whole been kind to the *Allegro de concert*. The earliest review – that of Maurice Bourges, in 1842 – highlighted its potential 'to satisfy a larger audience': 'The majestic introduction, the first melody in A major, the melodic developments that follow, above all the light and brilliant figuration in E major, which serves as the basis of the rest of the piece, are in a style universally well received, without however being vulgar.'[24] Schumann's response from the same year was less complimentary:

> The Concert-Allegro has entirely the form of a concerto first movement and probably was originally written with orchestral accompaniment. It lacks a lovely cantabile melody in the middle section, although it is rich in new and brilliant passagework; as it stands, it meanders restlessly. One feels the need for a slow movement to follow it, an Adagio, for the design as a whole suggests a complete concerto in three movements.[25]

Niecks expressed similar views almost fifty years later, referring to 'passages which are more distinctly orchestral than anything Chopin ever wrote for the orchestra'. The tuttis, however, have 'the heaviness of an arrangement', while the solo parts convey 'Chopin's usual airiness'. He states: 'The work, as a whole, is unsatisfactory, nay, almost indigestible. The subjects are neither striking nor important. Of the passage-work, that which follows the second subject contains the most interesting matter. Piquant traits and all sorts of fragmentary beauties are scattered here and there over the movement.' But overall it 'adds little or nothing to the value of our Chopin inheritance'.[26]

Referring explicitly to Niecks (yet again, the benchmark critic throughout this century), Huneker also asserts that the work 'adds little to Chopin's reputation', although 'it has the potentialities of a powerful and more manly composition than either of the two concertos'. He regards it as 'one of Chopin's most difficult works', abounding in 'risky skips' and 'ambuscades of dangerous double notes', its expressive content 'strikingly adapted for public performance'.[27] In the same vein, G. C. Ashton Jonson expresses astonishment that the *Allegro de concert* was 'so neglected by modern *virtuosi*; nothing that Liszt has written surpasses it in pianistic brilliance; it is difficult enough to make it interesting even to the greatest technician, and it gives scope for the highest artistic intelligence in its rendering'. He also considers the second theme 'exceedingly characteristic of Chopin's earlier period',[28] a point echoing Leichtentritt's assumption on the basis of stylistic evidence that Op. 46 dated from not long after the two concertos, if only in sketch form.[29] Weissmann discerns in the piece a Pyrrhic victory after fierce struggle,[30] Scharlitt a pianistic Procrustean bed.[31] Zdislas Jachimecki views it as 'a provisional sketch of a piano and orchestra piece whose instrumentation was to have been effected at a later date',[32] while Cortot expresses gratitude that 'it was in a sufficiently advanced stage of completion for [Jean-Louis] Nicodé eventually to make a passable version for piano and orchestra'.[33] The work struck Jachimecki as partly motivated by 'material factors', a point echoed by Weinstock: 'The thrifty Chopin had simply allowed the late publication of early materials, thus earning some much-needed francs. The music clearly shows that it had been conceived in connection with his long-discarded intention to shine as a piano virtuoso.'[34]

More generous assessments have emerged in recent years. Notwithstanding 'transparent inconsistencies of style', Peter Gould finds the *Allegro de concert* 'an absorbing and indeed fascinating work . . . with many examples of superb inspiration and blazing originality'.[35] Samson dubs it 'a fascinating and teasing work in the Chopin canon', 'one whose virtuosity exceeds almost anything else' by the composer.[36] He also claims:

> it has special interest as the only one of Chopin's concerto [first] movements to adhere to a more-or-less conventional tonal scheme. There is a monotonal prelude, a first solo presenting song (new material) and bravura pattern in the tonic, followed by a second subject and bravura pattern in the dominant. After the second ritornello the second solo presents an elaborated, nocturne-like version of the second subject in the tonic minor, there is further bravura writing and a closing ritornello linked thematically to the prelude.[37]

However conventional its tonal scheme, the work's formal plan was found wanting by Nicodé, whose much-expanded arrangements[38] for orchestra and for two pianos insert a full-blown development section after bar 205, a third tutti, a recapitulation of the piano's first theme (elided in Chopin's original), a transposition of the first *Spielepisode* (from bars 105ff.), and a reprise of the second theme in the tonic, which picks up from Chopin's bar 216. The purpose of all this is to 'standardise' the work according to a textbook sonata-form model, an act deplored by Niecks and others. Nicodé also beefs up the piano part at the end, whereas Kazimierz Wiłkomirski's orchestration from the early 1930s downplays the soloist in favour of the accompaniment – ironically so, given that this solo-piano concerto eliminates any risk of the orchestral domination previously experienced by Chopin. Although it corresponds to the solo version in form, there is much new instrumental writing, including a canonic cello obbligato at bars 200ff. and triangle highlights on the downbeats of bars 228ff.

Wiłkomirski's arrangement is played by Michael Ponti with the Berlin Symphony Orchestra on Vox CDX 5064, one of few commercial recordings of the *Allegro de concert*, even in 'complete' series.[39] Among the solo performances on record, Claudio Arrau's (Columbia 33CX 1443, from 1956) is particularly well conceived, logically proceeding from the pianistically treated 'orchestral' introduction – shaped with rubato, imbued with lyricism – to the rhythmically alive 'finale', which starts *dolce* but gradually develops momentum while remaining light in touch. One's principal complaint is that the initial 'slow 2' (in keeping with the time signature in most editions, ₵) lapses into four beats per bar, whereas Nikita Magaloff's performance (Philips 6768067/6542419, from the late 1970s) is in 𝄴 throughout, but at an over-slow tempo that makes the music sound leaden and ponderous. Roger Woodward's (HMV HQS 1303, from 1973) has even less impulse, his tempo structure also lacking the consistency of Magaloff's, while Barbara Hesse-Bukowska offers a stylistically admirable rendition (Muza XL0079, from ca 1958) characterised by light and pearly virtuosity within a 'vital' temporal and dynamic framework. But Arrau's interpretation is more magisterial, achieving the balance between nostalgic regret and heroic triumph that might have characterised Chopin's own performance in 'a free Warsaw'.

Re-evaluation

Scholarly preoccupation with the *Allegro de concert*'s chronology and 'stylistic inconsistencies' has diverted attention from its 'profound effect' when actualised in sound – as in the case of Op. 11 and Op. 21, although for different reasons. The work's tonal structure is straightforward, modulating from the tonic A major through the dominant back to the tonic via its parallel, A minor. This simple progression supports successive 'tutti' and 'solo' sections as follows: T_1, bars 1–87; S_1, bars 91–181, after a four-bar lead-in at the end of T_1; T_2, bars 182–99; S_2, bars 200–27, the piano re-entering with a flourish in bar 199; 'finale', bars 228–67; T_3, bar 268–end, with interjections from the keyboard. The chief difference from the first movements of Op. 11 and Op. 21 lies in the second solo's truncation (there is no 'working-out' section) and the elision of much of the recapitulation after the second solo – hence Nicodé's adjustments.

This formal scheme corresponds to the alternating pattern typical of the *stile brillante*. The introductory T_1 – marked 'Allegro maestoso' as in Op. 11, but in certain respects more like a French operatic overture[40] than a concerto tutti – opens with a non-recurrent theme (1a), building towards climax by means of two rhythmic motifs used frequently hereafter, ♩♩♩♩ ♪ and (7) ♩♩♩ | ♩. After timpani-like punctuation, the

Example 5.1 Op. 46, bars 120–4: harmonic foundation

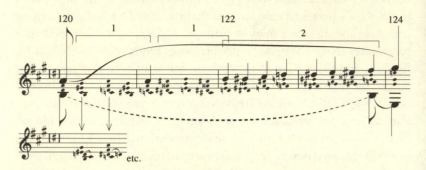

more processive second theme enters in bar 41 in A major, eventually followed by a triumphant closing theme in bars 65ff. later heard in T_2 and T_3. The music then winds down in a coda-like passage preparing the solo's entrance in bar 87, its initially reticent 'cadenza' followed by emphatic establishment of the tonic.[41] The first solo proper begins with another non-recurrent theme (1b) more pianistic in nature than its 'tutti' counterpart, this pattern corresponding to Op. 21. Lavishly ornamented, the theme bears a vague resemblance to some in the concertos (compare bar 97 with bar 37 in the Romance), but the mood is more confident, even bombastic, as in the surprisingly forthright cadential emphasis in bar 98. Another distinctive feature occurs in bars 103–4, where Chopin launches into right-hand octaves not to shadow the melody with a second 'voice' but to add pianistic force. The *Spielepisode* in bars 105ff. is also more overtly virtuosic than those in Op. 11 and Op. 21, although its seamless preparation recalls the latter. Chopin's familiar phraseology is employed, with short units preceding larger gestures immediately after. For instance, bars 109–14 break down to 1 + 1 + 4, the final part an extension serving to reinforce V of V, which is the underlying harmony throughout the episode notwithstanding the extraordinary surface complexity at times (as in the highly unusual bars 120–3, dissected in Example 5.1). Here Chopin pushes ahead to E major (V), where theme 2 enters in soloistic garb for the first time.

Despite occasional *fioriture* and turns, the theme (forming an asymmetrical period of 16 + 10 bars) generally remains simple, growing in

Example 5.2 Op. 46, bars 145–50[1]

tension in its second, shorter phrase with a Lisztian 'crescendo' in octaves (Example 5.2) – another keyboard trait atypical of the concertos and Chopin's music in general.[42] Superficially, the *Spielepisode* that follows resembles those of earlier 'brilliant' pieces, but its all-embracing chromatic foundation is more enterprising. After two statements of an inconsequential four-bar idea, Chopin embarks on three successive sequences, ascending chromatically from E major to F♯ minor in the first (bars 158–61); then through G♯ minor, A minor, B♭ minor, B minor and C minor in the second (all within two bars,[43] in harmonic 'acciaccaturas' analogous to those in bars 175–8, 246–7 and 256–9); and finally through C♯ minor and D♯ minor (bars 164–7). After a two-bar diminished-seventh interruption, the passage's E major goal is weakly attained, to be reinforced in a momentum-generating conclusion in which the multiple trills in bars 179–81 and accompanying 'timpani' punctuation herald T_2's commencement in bar 182.

At this point the triumphant 'closing theme' returns; developmentally treated, it ends with a series of juxtaposed chords (bars 190–1; compare bars 226–7) and then material from T_1 previously used to prepare the second theme. As before, the theme enters just after, but

Example 5.3 Op. 46, bars 221–4

transposed to the parallel minor in a moment of introspection, its hollow melancholy anticipating a similar moment in the E major Scherzo Op. 54 (bars 393ff.). Soon the mood brightens, however, and in bar 216 theme 2 is restored to A major, texturally enhanced and registrally expansive in a characteristic 'apotheosis'.[44] Employing another Lisztian 'crescendo' (Example 5.3), the music eventually embarks on the 'finale' in bar 228. Initially gentle, this concluding passage builds in intensity and technical difficulty towards the 'tutti' eruption in bar 268, the 'closing theme' now provoking a last outburst from the soloist. One can almost hear the audience in 'a free Warsaw' breaking into applause after the cascading double octaves in bars 276–7.

This image may indeed have been in Chopin's mind as he completed the *Allegro de concert* in 1841. While its compositional genesis remains obscure, the finished work's potential effect on listeners is perfectly obvious, generated by such devices as powerful octaves, 'risky skips' and 'dangerous double notes' – all of which reflect a more virtuosic keyboard technique than that required by Chopin's other music, including the two concertos. Some of these features may simply have resulted from his writing a *third* virtuoso concerto – moreover, a virtuoso concerto in a major key, which necessarily engaged a musical vocabulary inappropriate for use in a minor-key work like Op. 11 or Op. 21. But other features are less easily explained.

It must be remembered that Chopin's aspirations as a composer-pianist were pinned squarely on the E minor Concerto, his Paris warhorse; later, he came to view it with nostalgia, its hold still potent many years after he last performed it in Paris in April 1835.[45] Sowiński's account rings true of a Chopin distressed and dismayed by the incomprehension that greeted his concerto both then and earlier, caused in part by the incompatibility of his unique performance style and the instrumental forces accompanying him.[46] It is possible that his appetite for publishing a 'third concerto' – apparently ready for release as early as 1834, at least in part – vanished in the wake of his 1835 failure (as he perceived it), but that, some six years later, at a 'respectable distance' from Op. 21's publication in 1836, and prompted by admiration for his 'cherished disciple' Müller, he responded to earlier disappointments by moulding from his planned concerto a solo piece in which his technical prowess and *bel canto* sound alike could be projected without risk of compromise, a work destined 'to satisfy a larger audience', 'in a style universally well received'. At this later date, he could of course draw upon a Lisztian virtuoso idiom and fully exploit the formal procedures refined in his own music during the 1830s (among them the apotheosis principle) in order to achieve the resounding success – the 'profound effect' – denied to him in 1835 and before. Furthermore, that Chopin should have wanted to save his triumphant return to the concert stage for his return to 'a free Warsaw' seems entirely appropriate: not only might he have furthered the Polish cause on that occasion,[47] but he would have realised personal ambitions and achieved a kind of homecoming longed for since leaving Poland in November 1830, shortly after the E minor's debut.

This explanation may of course be nothing more than an extravagant fiction like the many surrounding Op. 11 and Op. 21 and those in the Chopin 'legend' more generally. Perhaps it would be safer simply to acknowledge the *Allegro de concert's* hidden virtues – formal ingenuity, technical innovations, careful pacing, strategic emotional contrasts – all of which justify a more favourable response than the one it has had during the past 150 years. But such a 'fiction' is precisely the sort of narrative performers construct as a guide to their playing, alongside a conscious or unconscious sense of musical narratives like the ones traced in this book. To that extent, it may be a legitimate interpretation, sure to be superseded in due course, but for the time being enlightening some aspect of the music's elusive meaning while leaving space for fresh evaluations to come.

Appendices

1 Reviews of Chopin's performances

F minor Concerto

Warsaw, 3 March 1830 (rehearsal)
Powszechny dziennik krajowy, 4 March 1830
Kurier warszawski, 5 March 1830

Warsaw, 17 March 1830
Gazeta warszawska, 18 March 1830
Kurier polski, 18 March 1830
Kurier warszawski, 18 March 1830
Gazeta korespondenta warszawskiego i zagranicznego, 19 March 1830
Powszechny dziennik krajowy, 19 March 1830
Kurier polski, 20 March 1830
Pamiętnik dla płci pięknej (Warsaw 1830), II/1:46

Warsaw, 22 March 1830
Kurier warszawski, 23 March 1830
Kurier polski, 24 March 1830
Powszechny dziennik krajowy, 25 March 1830
Kurier polski, 26 March 1830

E minor Concerto

Warsaw, 22 September 1830 (rehearsal)
Kurier warszawski, 23 September 1830
Powszechny dziennik krajowy, 24 September 1830

Warsaw, 11 October 1830
Kurier warszawski, 12 October 1830

Vienna, 11 June 1831
Allgemeine Theaterzeitung, 18 June 1831
Wiener Zeitung für Kunst, Literatur, Theater und Mode, 27 June 1831

Munich, 28 August 1831
Flora, 30 August 1831

Paris, 26 February 1832
Revue musicale, 3 March 1832

Paris, 20 May 1832, first movement
Revue musicale, 26 May 1832

Paris, 14 December 1834, second movement
Le Pianiste, 20 December 1834
Gazette musicale, 28 December 1834
Le Rénovateur, 5 January 1835

Paris, 5 April 1835
Gazette musicale, 12 April 1835
Neue Zeitschrift für Musik, 24 April 1835
Kronika emigracji polskiej, 29 April 1835

Rouen, 12 March 1838
Echo de Rouen, 13 March 1838
Journal de Rouen, 13 March 1838
Revue et Gazette musicale de Paris, 25 March 1838

2 Select editions

Piano solo

first editions

Op. 11   Schlesinger, Paris, June 1833 (plate no. 1409)
          Kistner, Leipzig, September 1833 (plate nos. 1020, 1021, 1022)
          Wessel, London, May 1834? (plate no. 1086)

Op. 21   Breitkopf & Härtel, Leipzig, April 1836 (plate no. 5654)
          Wessel, London, May 1836 (plate no. 1642)
          Schlesinger, Paris, July–September 1836 (plate no. 1940)

later versions of first editions

Op. 11   Kistner, Leipzig, ca 1858 (plate nos. 1020, 1021, 1022, 2340)
Op. 21   Breitkopf & Härtel, Leipzig, ca 1860 (plate no. 5654)
both   Ashdown & Parry [Wessel], London, after 1860 (plate nos. 1086 and
          1642)

collected editions

Richault, Paris, 1860, ed. Tellefsen
Schonenberger, Paris, 1860, ed. Fétis
Stellowsky, St Petersburg, 1861
Heugel, Paris, 1862–3, ed. Marmontel
Gebethner & Wolff, Warsaw, ca 1863–5
Jurgenson, Moscow, ca 1873, ed. Klindworth
Peters, Leipzig, 1879, ed. Scholtz
Schlesinger, Berlin, ca 1880–5 and Schirmer, New York, 1884, ed. Kullak
Steingräber, Leipzig, 1885, ed. Mertke
Durand, Paris, 1915–16, ed. Debussy
Oxford University Press, Oxford, 1932, ed. Ganche
Polskie Wydawnictwo Muzyczne, Cracow, 1980, ed. Ekier (Op. 21)

With second-piano reduction of orchestral accompaniment

Op. 11   Kistner, Leipzig, ca 1852–9, ed. Enke
Op. 21   Breitkopf & Härtel, Leipzig, ca 1860–4, ed. Horn
          Polskie Wydawnictwo Muzyczne, Cracow, 1985, ed. Ekier
both   Richault, Paris, 1860, ed. Tellefsen
          Kistner, Leipzig, 1879, ed. Mikuli
          Polskie Wydawnictwo Muzyczne, Cracow, 1958, ed. Paderewski,
          Bronarski and Turczyński

Henle, Munich, 1989 (Op. 11) and 1993 (Op. 21), ed. Zimmermann
Peters, London, forthcoming 1999, ed. Rink

Orchestral

Op. 11   Kistner, Leipzig, ca 1865–8
Eulenburg, London, 1985, ed. Stegemann
Op. 21   Breitkopf & Härtel, Leipzig, ca 1865–6
both   Breitkopf & Härtel, Leipzig, 1879 (Op. 21) and 1880 (Op. 11), ed. Brahms
Eulenburg, London, 1957, ed. Askenase
Polskie Wydawnictwo Muzyczne, Cracow, 1960, ed. Sikorski

Transcriptions and arrangements

reorchestrations

Op. 11   Ries, Berlin, ca 1880, arr. Tausig
Zimmermann, Leipzig, ca 1910, arr. Balakirev
Op. 21   Jurgenson, Moscow, 1878, arr. Klindworth
Heugel, Paris, n.d., arr. Messager

other

Op. 11   piano four-hands, arr. Schubert (Kistner, Leipzig, ca 1841)
quintet accompaniment, arr. Hofmann (Kistner, Leipzig, ca 1875)
Allegro maestoso and Romance – piano, arr. Fisher (Peters-Hinrichsen, London, 1950)
Romance – violin and piano, arr. Wilhelmj (Kistner, Leipzig, ca 1870)
    – piano, arr. Balakirev (Zimmermann, Leipzig, ca 1905)
Op. 21   mazurkas and waltzes for piano, comp. Orłowski (Brzezina, Warsaw, 1830)
piano four-hands, arr. Schubert (Breitkopf & Härtel, Leipzig, ca 1841)
quintet accompaniment, arr. Waldersee (Breitkopf & Härtel, Leipzig, ca 1875)
Maestoso – cadenza, comp. Burmeister (Schuberth, Leipzig, ca 1892–7)
Larghetto – piano, arr. Reinecke (Breitkopf & Härtel, Leipzig, ca 1870)
    – violin and piano, arr. Wilhelmj (Breitkopf & Härtel, Leipzig, ca 1870)
    – solo voices, vocal quartet and organ, arr. Schnecker (Schuberth, London, 1903)

3 Select discography

Op. 11

Alexander Brailowsky, Berlin Philharmonic Orchestra, cond. Julius Prüwer, 1928 (Polydor 66753–6)

Moriz Rosenthal, Berlin Opera Orchestra, cond. Friedrich Weissmann, 1931 (Parlophone 9558–9/B 12451–3)

Artur Rubinstein, London Symphony Orchestra, cond. John Barbirolli, 1937 (HMV DB 3201–4)

Josef Hofmann, New York Philharmonic Orchestra, cond. John Barbirolli, 1938 (IPL 502)

Raoul Koczalski, RIAS Orchestra Berlin, cond. Sergiu Celibidache, 1948? (unreleased)

Dinu Lipatti, Zurich Tonhalle-Orchester, cond. Otto Ackermann, 1948 (EMI CZS 7 671632)

Mieczysław Horszowski, Vienna State Opera Orchestra, cond. Hans Swarowsky, 1952 (Vox PL 7870)

Friedrich Gulda, London Philharmonic Orchestra, cond. Adrian Boult, 1954 (Decca LXT 2925)

Artur Rubinstein, Los Angeles Philharmonic Orchestra, cond. Alfred Wallenstein, 1954 (Vic LM–1810)

Fou Ts'ong, National Philharmonic Orchestra, cond. Zdzisław Górzyński, 1955 (Pathé 33 DTX 173)

Alexander Brailowsky, RCA Victor Symphony Orchestra, cond. William Steinberg, 1957 (HMV ALP 1015)

Halina Czerny-Stefańska, Czech Philharmonic Orchestra, cond. Vaclav Smetáček, 1958 (Supraphon SUA 10130)

Adam Harasiewicz, Vienna Symphony Orchestra, cond. Heinrich Hollreiser, 1958 (Philips 422 472–2)

Maurizio Pollini, Philharmonia, cond. Paul Kletzki, 1960 (ALP 1794)

Rosina Lhévinne, New York Philharmonic Orchestra, cond. Leonard Bernstein, 1963 (NSA 774)

Marta Argerich, London Symphony Orchestra, cond. Claudio Abbado, 1968 (DG 139 383)

Garrick Ohlsson, Romance arr. Balakirev for piano solo, 1974 (Desmar DSM 1005)

Emmanuel Ax, Philadelphia Orchestra, cond. Eugene Ormandy, 1978 (RCA RD 85317)

Krystian Zimerman, Los Angeles Philharmonic Orchestra, cond. Carlo Maria Giulini, 1978 (DG 2531 125)

Bella Davidovich, London Symphony Orchestra, cond. Neville Marriner, 1979 (Philips 9500 889)

Evgeny Kissin, Moscow Philharmonic Orchestra, cond. Dmitri Kitaenko, 1984 (RCA 09026 683782)

Murray Perahia, Israel Philharmonic Orchestra, cond. Zubin Mehta, 1989 (Sony SK 44922)

Nikolai Demidenko, Philharmonia, cond. Heinrich Schiff, 1993 (Hyperion CDA 66647)

Fumiko Shiraga, The Yggdrasil Quartet with Jan-Inge Haukås, 1996 (BIS-CD-847)

Op. 21

Marguerite Long, Paris Conservatoire Orchestra, cond. Philippe Gaubert, 1930 (Col LX 4–7)

Artur Rubinstein, London Symphony Orchestra, cond. John Barbirolli, 1931 (HMV DB 1494–7)

Alfred Cortot, unidentified orchestra, cond. John Barbirolli, 1935 (HMV DB 2612–15)

Josef Hofmann, New York Philharmonic Orchestra, cond. John Barbirolli, 1937 (IPL 501)

Raoul Koczalski, Berlin Philharmonic Orchestra, cond. Sergiu Celibidache, 1948 (Rococo RR 2095)

Vladimir Ashkenazy, National Philharmonic Orchestra, cond. Zdzisław Górzyński, 1955 (Pathé DTX 172)

Stefan Askenase, Berlin Philharmonic Orchestra, cond. Fritz Lehmann, 1955 (DGM 18040)

Clara Haskil, Orchestre des Concerts Lamoureux, cond. Igor Markevitch, 1955 (Philips A02075L)

Marguerite Long, Orchestre de la Société des Concerts du Conservatoire, cond. André Cluytens, 1955 (Angel GR–2216)

Guiomar Novaes, Vienna Symphony Orchestra, cond. Otto Klemperer, 1950s (Vox PL 11.380)

Artur Rubinstein, National Philharmonic Orchestra, cond. Witold Rowicki, 1960 (Muza SX 1861)

Marta Argerich, National Symphony Orchestra of Washington, cond. Mstislav Rostropovich, 1978 (DGG 2531 042)

Krystian Zimerman, Los Angeles Philharmonic Orchestra, cond. Carlo Maria Giulini, 1979 (DGG 2531 126)

Evgeny Kissin, Moscow Philharmonic Orchestra, cond. Dmitri Kitaenko, 1984 (RCA 09026 683782)

Murray Perahia, Israel Philharmonic Orchestra, cond. Zubin Mehta, 1989 (Sony SK 44922)

Melvyn Tan, London Classical Players, cond. Roger Norrington, 1989 (NSA B4432)

Nikolai Demidenko, Philharmonia, cond. Heinrich Schiff, 1993 (Hyperion CDA 66647)

Fumiko Shiraga, The Yggdrasil Quartet with Jan-Inge Haukås, 1996 (BIS-CD-847)

Notes

1 Contexts

1 Walter Benjamin's phrase. For discussion of cultural life in early nineteenth-century Paris, see Bloom (ed.), *Music in Paris*, and Ralph P. Locke, 'Paris: centre of intellectual ferment', in Ringer (ed.), *Early Romantic*, 32–83. Sachs ('London') also provides relevant background information.

2 His praise for Chopin's Variations on 'Là ci darem la mano' ('Ein Opus II', *Allgemeine musikalische Zeitung* 33 (1831), cols. 805–8) could not have been more fulsome, however. Leon Plantinga (*Schumann as Critic* (New Haven 1967), 196–218) explores Schumann's reaction to the virtuoso 'cult'.

3 See Robert Wangermée, 'Tradition et innovation dans la virtuosité romantique', *Acta musicologica* 42 (1970), 5–32.

4 See Janet Ritterman, 'Piano music and the public concert, 1800–1850', in Samson (ed.), *Cambridge Companion*, 11–31 and 296–301.

5 For discussion see Dahlhaus, *Nineteenth-Century Music*, 140–2; also, Amster, *Virtuosenkonzert*, and Frączkiewicz, 'Koncerty'. General histories of the concerto appear in Engel, *Instrumentalkonzert*; Robert Layton (ed.), *A Companion to the Concerto* (London 1988); Roeder, *History*; and Schering, *Geschichte*.

6 Tovey observes that the concerto's main purpose is not soloistic display, but the creation of a dialogue between competing parts ('The classical concerto', in *Essays*, 6–14).

7 Stevens ('Theme') traces the evolution of theoretical concerto models. See also Scott L. Balthazar, 'Intellectual history and concepts of the concerto: some parallels from 1750 to 1850', *Journal of the American Musicological Society* 36 (1983), 39–72.

8 Stevens, 'Theme', 47, 48.

9 For elaboration see Samson, *Four Ballades*, *Master Musicians* and *Music of Chopin*.

10 Chomiński, *Chopin*, 59. All translations are mine unless otherwise indicated.

11 See Dahlhaus, *Nineteenth-Century Music*, 125–34, and Gerhard, 'Ballade', 117–19 and 121–5.

12 Julian Rushton, *Classical Music* (London 1986), 171. Sachs ('London', 207) explores 'the chief difference between the aria and concerto cults'.

13 For summaries of Chopin's Warsaw years, see Chomiński, *Chopin*; Kobylańska, *Chopin*; and Tomaszewski and Weber, *Chopin*.

14 Amster, *Virtuosenkonzert*.

15 See Rink, 'Evolution', 63–4, and 'Tonal architecture', 307–8 n. 22.

16 Chomiński (*Chopin*, 9–17) and Smialek (*Dobrzyński*, 12–22) outline early nineteenth-century Polish history.

17 For further information about music available in early nineteenth-century Warsaw, see Smialek, *Dobrzyński*, 16, and Maria Prokopowicz, 'Musique imprimée à Varsovie en 1800–1830', in Lissa (ed.), *Book*, 593–7.

18 Kobylańska (*Chopin*, 151–9 and 207–13) provides details of virtuoso concerts in Warsaw from 1827 to 1830.

19 Eigeldinger ('Placing Chopin') investigates Chopin's eighteenth-century aesthetic orientation.

20 See Eigeldinger, *Chopin: Pianist*.

21 See Chomiński, *Chopin*, 32ff., and Samson, *Master Musicians*, 51ff.

22 Chomiński (*Chopin*, 45) notes that Chopin composed his works with orchestral accompaniment while still in Warsaw, under Elsner's watchful eye.

23 *Allgemeine Theaterzeitung*, Vienna, 20 August 1829; translation from Atwood, *Chopin*, 200. Other reviews of Chopin's Vienna concerts appear in Atwood, 201–4.

24 See Rink, 'Evolution'.

25 Samson's term (*Four Ballades*, 4).

26 Compare the classifications in Rink, 'Tonal architecture', 80, and Samson, *Four Ballades*, 5.

27 Rink ('Evolution' and 'Tonal architecture') examines Chopin's developing compositional technique during the Warsaw and early Paris years.

28 See Rink, 'Tonal architecture', 88ff.

29 Chomiński, *Chopin*, 59.

2 Creation

1 Chopin, *Selected Correspondence*, 36.

2 Ibid., 40.

3 Ibid., 45. Certain details have been changed in accordance with the original.

4 Ibid., 57, 58.

5 Both concertos are scored for pairs of flutes, oboes, clarinets, bassoons and

trumpets, plus timpanis and strings. In addition, the F minor has two horns and bass trombone; the E minor, four horns and trombone.

6 The sketch sheet is reproduced in Kobylańska, *Chopin*, 194. See Wróblewska-Straus, 'Manuscrits', 161–4 for discussion and a facsimile of Fontana's accompaniment.

7 Its presence in Breitkopf's archive (now in the Biblioteka Narodowa, Warsaw) indicates that it had this function (see Kobylańska, *Rękopisy*, I:117–21, and Kallberg, 'Chopin', 799 n. 3), as do Chopin's handwritten instructions to the printer (such as 'il faut graver ces notes en petit', concerning the *fioriture* in bars 273 and 275 of the Maestoso). Wróblewska-Straus ('Manuscrits', 164) states categorically that the partial autograph – notated on French paper watermarked 'BLACONS', dating from ca 1835 – was the *Stichvorlage* for the German first edition. Chopin's use of a copyist to transcribe the parts (arranged timpani, brass, winds, upper strings, piano, lower strings) is understandable, given the confusion that had occurred in Vienna in 1829 (see p. 13).

   Note that Kobylańska's putative 'autograph sketch' (*Rękopisy*, I:117) was for the 'Lento con gran espressione', not the F minor Concerto (cf. Chomiński and Turło, *Katalog*, 106); as hypothetical sources, Dobrzyński's manuscripts (*Rękopisy*, I:93, 121; see Chapter 4, n. 49) and autograph reductions for quartet or quintet (*Rękopisy*, I:94, 123) are equally implausible.

8 Chomiński and Turło (*Katalog*, 102) assert that Franchomme intended his accompaniment as a corrective to Tellefsen's 1860 Richault edition (see p. 32). They also describe an unusual handwritten orchestral score in Prague of uncertain date (ibid., 102–3).

9 This was Chopin's only public appearance in Vienna during this period. According to Szalsza ('Wiener Konzerte'; see also Piotr Szalsza, 'Koncert, którego nie było. Poprawka do biografii Chopina', *Ruch muzyczny* 30/6 (1986), 17–20), the benefit concert of Mme Garcia-Vestris advertised for 4 April 1831, in which Chopin was to play the E minor Concerto, did not take place, contrary to most biographical accounts.

10 The programme (reproduced in Roeder, *History*, 223) indicates that the *Fantasy on Polish Airs*, which ended the concert, was played with orchestra.

11 Details of this and the principal Paris performances are provided in Eigeldinger, 'Premiers concerts'; see also Eigeldinger, 'Un concert inconnu de Chopin à Paris', *Revue musicale de Suisse romande* 34 (1981), 2–9. Chopin might have performed the concerto without accompaniment in Rouen, but the presence of Spohr's Nonet on the programme suggests otherwise. (See the *Echo de Rouen*, 12 March 1838; compare the *Echo de Rouen* and *Journal de*

Rouen of 13 March 1838.) Chopin also played the E minor Concerto before the celebrated pianist Kalkbrenner in November 1831.

12 Eigeldinger, 'Premiers concerts', 257. The misunderstanding about the F minor stems from Chopin's comment in a letter to Tytus of 12 December 1831 regarding his planned debut concert on 25 December (postponed until February), namely, 'I shall play my F minor Concerto and my Variations in B♭ [Op. 2]' (Chopin, *Selected Correspondence*, 99). Incidentally, Eigeldinger ('Premiers concerts', 261–2 n. 40) infers from this and other letters that the F minor's orchestral parts were available for performance (see p. 20); he also assumes that the participation of Baillot's quintet in the first half of the 26 February concert and the lack of references to an orchestra in the review point to Chopin's own use of the quintet for his concerto (see Eigeldinger, 263–4).

13 Clara Wieck's diary (see n. 29 below) indicates that Chopin had previously performed the work on 14 March 1832 at Abbé Bertin's, probably accompanied by strings (Mendelssohn's Octet was also played). I am grateful to Jeffrey Kallberg and Claudia Macdonald for this information.

14 According to Eigeldinger ('Premiers concerts', 271), 'Rondo' implies that the E minor was played. Chopin's hitherto unknown performance of 'un magnifique concerto' at a Schlesinger soirée on 16 February 1834 also deserves mention. Berlioz's account, in *Le Rénovateur* of 23 February 1834, describes a piece more like the eventual *Allegro de concert* Op. 46 than either of Chopin's concertos; see Chapter 5, n. 10. (Jean-Jacques Eigeldinger helpfully informed me of this event.)

15 Chopin's reaction to the concert on 5 April 1835 is documented in Albert Sowiński, *Les Musiciens polonais et slaves anciens et modernes* (Paris 1857), 116 (see Eigeldinger, 'Premiers concerts', 281; Samson, *Master Musicians*, 128; and Chapter 5 below):

> The famous Habeneck conducted the orchestra, the hall was full, everything went well; but, whether the public did not understand his work, whether a concerto in a large hall always leaves listeners a bit cold, Chopin's expectations were wrong in any case: his magnificent concerto did not at all have the desired effect. This miscalculation caused Chopin genuine distress; for a long time he did not want to play in public, and his aversion to playing in concerts dates from this time.

Chopin did appear in the benefit concerts of other musicians during the 1830s, but, as Eigeldinger observes ('Premiers concerts', 288), his pattern was to play the music of other composers when part of a larger company, and the E minor Concerto when he was the focus of attention.

His letter of 14 February 1838 to the Baron de Trémont refers to a rehearsal of his 'concerto' (the key is unspecified) at the latter's apartments on the 16th, possibly in preparation for his impending concert at Louis-Philippe's Tuileries court (although a review of the concert – in the *Revue et Gazette musicale de Paris*, 25 February 1838 – fails to mention a concerto).

16 Chopin, *Selected Correspondence*, 38.

17 Translation from Atwood, *Chopin*, 209. The original is reproduced in Kobylańska, *Chopin*, 243 (see also 242 and 245).

18 Translation from Atwood, *Chopin*, 207.

19 Ibid., 211; certain details have been modified to conform to the original.

20 Ibid., 213, 215. The review of 24 March, by Maurycy Mochnacki, also compares Chopin's concerto 'to the life of a just man; no ambiguity, falsehood or exaggeration' (translation from Tomaszewski and Weber, *Chopin*, 68).

21 Translation from Atwood, *Chopin*, 216; italics in original (facsimile in Kobylańska, *Chopin*, 249; see also 248).

22 Chopin, *Selected Correspondence*, 54, 58.

23 Translation from Atwood, *Chopin*, 216 (facsimile in Kobylańska, *Chopin*, 263). The reviewer adds: 'The Adagio and Rondo were especially received with delight by all. The composer and virtuoso was overwhelmed by a wealth of applause and called back onstage after each solo.'

24 Chopin, *Selected Correspondence*, 60. The orchestra was conducted by Carlo Soliva.

25 Ibid., 62; the 'expert' may have been August Kahlert.

26 Translation from Atwood, *Chopin*, 217. The review (by F. A. Kanne) continues: 'although he has prepared a brilliant and impressive cadenza, some changes in it would seem desirable'. The *Wiener Zeitung*'s review of 27 June 1831 claimed: 'The composition had no special appeal, but the artist's playing met with deserved approbation' (quoted from Szalsza, 'Wiener Konzerte', 35).

27 Translation from Atwood, *Chopin*, 218.

28 Chopin, *Selected Correspondence*, 98; certain details have been changed in accordance with the original (cf. Chopin, *Korespondencja*, I:200).

29 Facsimile in Tomaszewski and Weber, *Chopin*, 103. Clara Wieck's diary account of the performance on 14 March 1832 at Abbé Bertin's (see n. 13 above) describes the concerto as 'just like Field': 'had I not known whose it was, I would have thought it a work of Schumann; it shouldn't be played before a mixed audience, for the virtuosity [*Passagen*] is novel, hugely difficult and not brilliant in the conventional manner'. (Quoted from Berthold Litzmann, *Clara Schumann: Ein Künstlerleben*, 3 vols. (Leipzig

1902–8), I:42. My thanks to Jeffrey Kallberg and Claudia Macdonald for this information.)

30 *Le Pianiste* also comments: 'In this too short fragment, M. Chopin showed that the simplest means, taste and grace, make a considerable impression on a worthy audience, and we can confirm that he was well appreciated [*bien compris*].'

31 In the *Gazette musicale* of 28 December 1834, 'P. R.' remarked that the movement 'is very well constructed and extremely rich in delicate nuances'.

32 Joseph Mainzer's laconic review of the concert (*Neue Zeitschrift für Musik*, 24 April 1835) makes no mention of Chopin; this in itself is telling, particularly as he was a sponsor. According to the *Kronika emigracji polskiej* of 29 April 1835: 'The [concert's] leading talents were magnificent, but dearest to us, shining among them, was our national . . . our Chopin' (translation from Tomaszewski and Weber, *Chopin*, 117).

33 The local press was also ecstatic, the *Echo de Rouen* (13 March 1838) exclaiming: 'To [Chopin] belonged all the evening's honours', while the *Journal de Rouen* (13 March) commented: 'his success was colossal', 'he *sings* at the piano, not striking the keys but flattering and caressing them'.

34 See Kallberg, 'Chopin'.

35 Eigeldinger, 'Premiers concerts', 262–3.

36 Kallberg ('Chopin') elaborates this point. Wessel adds 'Edited and Fingered by his Pupil A. Fontana [*sic*]' on the title and first pages.

37 Christophe Grabowski ('The original French editions of Fryderyk Chopin's music', *Chopin Studies* 4 (1994), Annex, 1–42) traces the complex history of Chopin's French first editions, concluding that certain variants in later impressions of the 'same' edition reflect the composer's intentions. (Grabowski also notes that numerous impressions of Op. 11 and Op. 21 were advertised at different prices in the *Revue et Gazette musicale de Paris* and the catalogues of Schlesinger and his successor, Brandus.) Variants similarly infiltrate later impressions of the German and English first editions, but in these cases Chopin's involvement is unlikely. Sample discrepancies between the original impressions of the first editions are adduced in Chapters 3 and 4.

38 See Kallberg, 'Chopin', and Eigeldinger, 'Premiers concerts'. Chapter 5 investigates epistolary references to a third concerto.

39 Mysteriously, the first editions of Op. 21 do not print wind and brass cues in the string parts for use by quartet or quintet accompaniment, even though these formats are specified respectively on the title pages of Schlesinger's and Breitkopf's editions. (Wessel indicates only solo and orchestral parts.) For instance, the wind responses in bars 2–3 and 4–5 of the Larghetto do not

appear in the string parts, likewise the 'Cor de signal' at bars 406ff. of the third movement. In the French and German first editions the dedicatee is Countess Delfina ('Delphine') Potocka; in the English first edition, 'Madame Anderson, de Londres'.

40 See Kallberg, 'Chopin', 560 and 569.

41 By 3 July 1835 Breitkopf had received a source for Op. 21 other than the partial autograph (identified as an 'ouvrage' in the receipt; see Kallberg, 'Chopin', 806 and 807); this might have been corrected proof sheets. An earlier autograph of at least the piano solo obviously existed at some point: in the Breitkopf manuscript – on paper from 1835 – Chopin entered the piano part *after* the orchestral instruments had been copied (see p. 14), indicating that it was transcribed from an earlier source.

42 Zimmermann ('Chopin', 179ff.) advances a similar but less ramified hypothesis. Another explanation, proposed by Jürgen Neubacher in private correspondence, is that the partial autograph was Breitkopf's principal *Stichvorlage*, German proof sheets or even the published score then being sent to Paris and London to serve as models for those editions, with Chopin's last-minute corrections introduced into the Schlesinger score. (Compare Ekier's analysis of the sources for Op. 27 No. 1 in his Polish National Edition of the Nocturnes, Annex, 10.)

43 Eigeldinger, 'Premiers concerts', 263.

44 Dubois' comment; translation from Eigeldinger, *Chopin: Pianist*, 63.

45 Mikuli's edition reproduces the first-movement variants, which include a melismatic turn and a *fioritura*. In Stirling's copy of the Romance, an arpeggiation embellishes bar 59's fermata (transcribed in Henle, 112), and in the score ostensibly used by Hartmann an extended scale leads to $c^{\sharp^4}$ in bar 59, followed by four $c^{\sharp^3}$s (marked 'loco') and then a diminished arpeggio in bar 61 (facsimile in Jean-Jacques Eigeldinger, *Chopin vu par ses élèves*, 3rd edn (Neuchâtel 1988), 321).

46 According to Jean-Jacques Eigeldinger, Chopin's Norwegian pupil Thomas Tellefsen – another guardian of his teaching tradition – entered some of the markings in Stirling's scores.

47 The foregoing discussion is based on Jean-Jacques Eigeldinger and Jean-Michel Nectoux, *Frédéric Chopin: œuvres pour piano. Fac-similé de l'exemplaire de Jane W. Stirling avec annotations et corrections de l'auteur* (Paris 1982), xxv–xxxiv passim; Eigeldinger, *Chopin: Pianist* (see his Appendix 2 for description of the annotated scores); and Eigeldinger's transcriptions of the Stirling and Dubois scores, which were generously shared with me. On the *cercar della nota*, see Eigeldinger, *Chopin: Pianist*, 114–15 n. 82, where additional instances of this in Op. 11 are cited.

48 Quoted from Eigeldinger, *Chopin: Pianist*, 53 (where examples of this 'accelerando principle' are provided from both concertos; see also ibid., 133 n. 127). Kleczyński also observed that Chopin's 'style is based upon simplicity, it admits of no affectation, and therefore does not allow too great changes of movement. This is an absolute condition for the execution of all Chopin's works and more especially of his Concertos; the richness and variety of the embellishments would tend to sickliness and affectation if the execution were not as simple as the conception.' (Quoted from ibid., 54.)

49 Eigeldinger's description, in ibid., 123 n. 106, where relevant examples are given.

50 These features are discussed in ibid., 107 n. 63, 108 n. 66, 113–14 n. 82, 117 n. 85, 121–2 n. 99, 131–3 n. 126 and 133–4 n. 128. See also Jean-Jacques Eigeldinger, 'Chopin et l'héritage baroque', *Schweizer Beiträge zur Musikwissenschaft* 2 (1974), 51–74.

51 Reviewed in *La France musicale* four days later and in *Der Humorist* on 23 February 1843. See Jean-Jacques Eigeldinger, 'Carl Filtsch, miroir de Chopin', in Francis Claudon (ed.), *La Fortune de Frédéric Chopin* (Paris 1994), 127–50 for discussion of this young prodigy, and for analysis of the spurious Filtsch letters included by Hedley in Chopin, *Selected Correspondence*.

52 Lenz, 'Uebersichtliche', 282–3; translation from Eigeldinger, *Chopin: Pianist*, 66–7. This account – in which Lenz also describes Chopin's nostalgia for the concerto ('"How I loved the piece! How I used to play it!" he said, as if to himself'; see Chapter 5, n. 45) – might relate to one of the 'séances d'artistes' reviewed in the *Revue et Gazette musicale de Paris*, 26 February 1843. Elsewhere (*Die grossen Pianoforte-Virtuosen unserer Zeit aus persönlicher Bekanntschaft. Liszt – Chopin – Tausig – Henselt* (Berlin 1872), 36), Lenz notes with disbelief Chopin's insistence that Filtsch played Op. 11 better than Chopin himself did.

53 Quoted from Eigeldinger, *Chopin: Pianist*, 67.

3 Interpretation

1 See Samson, 'Chopin reception', 2.

2 Compare Samson's judgement on the ballades (*Four Ballades*, 44).

3 Samson ('Chopin reception', 11) identifies a 'central paradox' in reception history: 'The more closely music approaches an autonomy character, the more susceptible it becomes to . . . appropriation.'

4 See John Rink, 'Chopin's ballades and the dialectic: analysis in historical perspective', *Music Analysis* 13 (1994), 99–115.

5 Samson, 'Chopin reception', 11.

6 Samson, *Four Ballades*, 34.

7 Samson, 'Chopin reception', 12.

8 Rellstab, 'Ueberblick der Erzeugnisse', *Iris im Gebiete der Tonkunst* 5 (1834), 89.

9 Fink, 'Recension', *Allgemeine musikalische Zeitung* 36 (1834), cols. 541, 542.

10 Davison, editorial response to correspondence, *The Musical World* 16 (1841), 309. In contrast, Davison's *An Essay on the Works of Frederic Chopin* (London [1843]) extravagantly describes the concertos as 'vast in their conception, bold in their outline, rich in their motivos, minutely and dexterously finished in their details' – 'only surpassed, if indeed they be surpassed, by those of the great Beethoven' (2).

11 *The Musical Magazine* 1 (1835), 111; italics in original.

12 Fink, 'Concerte für das Pianoforte', *Allgemeine musikalische Zeitung* 38 (1836), cols. 538, 539, 541.

13 Stoepel, 'Revue critique', *Gazette musicale* 1 (1834), 305, 306. Like all criticism, Stoepel's review – which appeared in the journal of the work's publisher, Schlesinger – is anything but neutral (see Samson, 'Chopin reception', 2).

14 Schumann, 'Friedrich Chopin', 138. On 3 May 1832, Schumann reported in his diary: 'The new concerto [in E minor] is novel, entirely noble, but full of tedious passages and oddities'. These impressions may be secondhand, as the work had not yet been published; compare Clara Wieck's comments, cited in Chapter 2, n. 29. Schumann also compares the status of Chopin's E minor Concerto to that of Berlioz's *Symphonie fantastique* ('Episode de la vie d'un Artiste', *Neue Zeitschrift für Musik* 3 (1835), 47). Berlioz himself dismissed the orchestral accompaniments in Chopin's concertos as 'cold and useless', all the interest being 'concentrated in the piano part' (*Mémoires de Hector Berlioz* (Paris 1878), 296).

15 Liszt, *F. Chopin* (Paris 1852), 10, 11.

16 Ehlert, *Aus der Tonwelt*, 2nd edn (Berlin 1882), 284, 293, 303, 305.

17 Lenz, 'Uebersichtliche', 282, 283.

18 Niecks, *Chopin*, I:205–12.

19 Here for the first time this henceforth ubiquitous criticism is voiced (I:211).

20 '[T]he first movement [of Op. 11] is too long, too much in one set of keys, and the working-out section too much in the nature of a technical study. The first movement of the F minor far transcends it in breadth, passion and musical feeling, but it is short and there is no coda . . . This concerto is altogether more human than the E minor' (Huneker, *Chopin*, 171).

21 Leichtentritt (*Chopin*, 39) attacks the concertos for their lack of symphonic, Beethovenian opposition between orchestra and piano, and their 'inade-

quate' developmental passages. He omits the concertos and other works with orchestra from his compendium of Chopin analyses (*Analyse der Chopin'schen Klavierwerke*, 2 vols. (Berlin 1921–2)), possibly because they conflict with his analytical aesthetic.

22 Branding them intimate 'Salon-Klavierkonzerte', Weissmann (*Chopin*, 169, 173) notes that changes in performing practice (steelier fingers, larger orchestras) magnified their weaknesses, although these were latent in the music, deriving from Chopin's soul.

23 According to Scharlitt (*Chopin*, 264, 266), orchestral writing was Chopin's Achilles heel; hence, the accompaniments in the concertos are 'anaemic'. Although both are immature, Op. 11 is richer, because written later, than Op. 21.

24 Op. 11 and Op. 21 are 'immature', 'poor examples of the piano concerto as such'; 'they must be considered purely and simply as large-scale show-pieces for the soloist, with necessary but regrettable orchestral back-grounds'. 'Chopin merely demonstrates that the beauties of key-relationship and key-balance perceived by all the Viennese classical masters meant nothing to him'; his 'weakness of key-sense was equalled only by the weakness of his sense of development' (Abraham, *Chopin's Musical Style*, 29, 36).

25 'It is the juvenile charm of the two concertos, the poetry of their slow move-ments and the brilliance of the piano writing that has kept them alive in spite of glaring weaknesses of construction' (Hedley, *Chopin*, 140).

26 Op. 11 'is a botched piece, the absence of which from the corpus of his works would not have diminished his position or present reputation at all'. In con-trast, Op. 21, 'despite mishandling, despite the changes of fashion, and despite not being "Chopin *in excelsis*" (Huneker), is a highly attractive work, superior in every detail to the E-minor' (Weinstock, *Chopin*, 197, 207).

27 Chopin's concertos 'may lack in great musical substance and true concerto drama', but they are 'eminently pianistic and contain a sufficient number of moments of melodic and pianistic magic to have kept them in the standard concerto repertory to this day . . . Both concertos suffer from problems. The orchestration is generally ineffective . . . Problems of tonal organization further mar the first movements . . . One common solution . . . has been to delete or significantly shorten the long and tedious opening tutti sections in modern performances. This creates no grave injustice to the music' (Roeder, *History*, 224, 225).

28 For instance, Tovey ('Chopin. Pianoforte Concerto in F minor, Op. 21', in *Essays*, 103–6 passim) remarks that Chopin 'is hampered by forms for which his training had given him no help'. 'The first movement of the E minor is

built on a suicidal plan which Chopin's adored master, Elssner [*sic*], must have at least approved if not actually taught.' In contrast, Op. 21, 'though not a powerfully organized work, has no fatal flaw; and its style is the perfection of ornament'. He also acknowledges that 'Chopin's orchestration, except for a solitary and unnecessary trombone part . . . and a few rectifiable slips, is an unpretentious and correct accompaniment to his pianoforte-writing'; furthermore, that the 'dramatic recitative' in Op. 21 'is as fine a piece of instrumentation as Berlioz could have chosen to quote in his famous treatise'. Each slow movement is 'a masterpiece in a form and a mood which neither Chopin nor any other composer reproduced later'.

Although Samson's critiques of the concertos are balanced, his *Music of Chopin* (40, 50, 54–6 passim) comments as follows: 'insecure grasp of the significance and power of tonal architecture'; 'failure to relate detail to whole'; 'the originality lies more in the detail than in the overall conception and formal mould'; 'it is the formal setting which disappoints', despite 'individual moments of ravishing beauty'. He concludes: 'In the end the concertos linger in the memory for the poetry of their detail rather than the strength of their structures', although 'the time has long passed when we needed to make an aggressive case in defence of Chopin's much-maligned scoring in the concertos. It is adequate to its purpose.'

29 Cortot (*In Search*, 55) writes that Op. 11 'presents, to a far greater extent than the F minor Concerto, an abundance of thorny problems in virtuosity that sometimes overlay the essential magnificence of the material employed'. (Compare Alfred Cortot, 'Deux concertos romantiques', *Conferencia* 31 (1937), 486–93.) In its 'Etude musicale analytique', the *Guide du Concert* (25 (1939), 403) also states that the piano part in Op. 11 is 'brilliantly treated, and if the melody has lost for musicians of our time something of its original flavour, the figuration has retained its elegance and the work still stands out by the splendour of its virtuosity'. In contrast, Gould ('Sonatas', 150, 151) observes that Op. 21's melodic decoration is 'thematic', not 'ornamental for its own sake', this 'fusion of the decorative with the substantial' recalling late Mozart – a point also suggested by Schumann, who observed that 'if a genius such as Mozart were born today, he would write concertos like Chopin's rather than Mozart's' (review of Taubert's Concerto Op. 18, *Neue Zeitschrift für Musik* 4 (1836), 115), and that in Chopin 'we find Mozart at the end of another path' ('Friedrich Chopin', 138).

30 For instance, Jachimecki (*Chopin*, 163) writes that Chopin's character permeates the concertos; Jan Kleczyński (*Frédéric Chopin: de l'interprétation de ses œuvres* (Paris [1880]), 8) discerns in them youth, exuberance, strength,

happiness, gaiety, and love of the world and humankind; while Maurycy Karasowski (*Frederic Chopin: His Life, Letters, and Works*, tr. Emily Hill, 2 vols. (London 1879), I:139) senses an 'inimitable youthful fire'.

31 For Schering (*Geschichte*, 187), Op. 11's form and character are archetypal, while Engel (*Instrumentalkonzert*, 333) writes: 'the concertos can be considered entirely typical of the brilliant–romantic concerto. The structure as a whole as well as most of the structural details are completely conventional. Even the themes are entirely consistent with the contemporary type.' Leon Plantinga also comments that Chopin's concerto structures are 'altogether standard among his own generation of pianist-composers' (*Romantic Music* (New York 1984), 194), a view shared by Zofia Lissa ('Fryderyk Chopin', in Hansjürgen Schaefer (ed.), *Konzertbuch: Orchestermusik A–F* (Berlin 1964), 397). Cf. however Frączkiewicz, 'Koncerty'.

32 Merkel, *Der Musikführer. Fréd. Chopin, Klavierkonzert in E-moll* (Frankfurt [1898]), 3.

33 Kretschmar, *Klavierkonzert in Emoll (Op. 11) von Fr. Chopin* (Leipzig 1902), 3, 4, 9, 14. Compare the diachronic breakdowns in Kretschmar's *Klavierkonzert Nr. 2 Fmoll (Op. 21) von Fr. Chopin* (Leipzig 1902); in Eduard Reuss, *Friedrich Chopin. Klavierkonzert in F moll. (Op. 21.)* (Berlin 1904); and in Zieliński, *Chopin*, 161–9 and 216–23.

34 See Samson, 'Chopin reception', 12.

35 This information, like much throughout this section and in Appendix 2, derives from Chomiński and Turło, *Katalog*, an exhaustive study of Chopin editions. See also Chechlińska, 'National Edition'.

36 Various Klindworth-influenced editions perpetuate this reading, e.g. Ricordi's of ca 1879–80, edited by Riccardo Vitali.

37 Surprisingly, Debussy follows suit – one of many instances where Scholtz (not Ignacy Friedman, as generally assumed) dictates his editorial decisions. Others are documented in Annie Dennis, 'Debussy's editing of Chopin' (M.Mus. diss., University of Surrey, 1992).

38 See p. 199 of the concertos volume.

39 See Jeffrey Kallberg, 'Are variants a problem? "Composer's intentions" in editing Chopin', *Chopin Studies* 3 (1990), 257–67.

40 These are outlined in Ekier's *Wstęp do Wydania Narodowego Dzieł Fryderyka Chopina* (Cracow 1974), and summarised in Chechlińska, 'National Edition'.

41 A volume of the concertos edited by the present author is forthcoming as part of *The Complete Chopin – A New Critical Edition*, published by Peters Edition London. Like Ekier's Op. 21, this reports variants on the page (their

provenance explicitly identified, however), but in general it follows a principal 'best source' rather than tacitly conflating within the main text. The result is *an* Urtext, rather than 'the' Urtext.

42　See Chomiński and Turło, *Katalog*, 104 and 107; cf. also Wróblewska-Straus, 'Manuscrits', 164. Comprehensive lists of second-piano reductions for both concertos are given in the former (348–9). Tellefsen's Op. 21 accompaniment is advertised in Richault's 1860 catalogue but may never have been published; in any case, no extant score can be found. (I am grateful to Christophe Grabowski for this information.)

43　Chomiński and Turło, *Katalog*, 104, 107.

44　See Samson, 'Chopin reception', 5–8 and 11.

45　In Brahms's edition, the soloist is then abandoned on a second-inversion tonic as the orchestra continues. (Here and throughout, the piano lacks the tutti reductions found in the manuscript and the earlier Breitkopf full score.)

46　Chomiński and Turło (*Katalog*, 348) list full-score editions of both concertos.

47　Two of Stegemann's five principal sources are incorrectly identified. His 'orchestral score' (xii) putatively published by Schlesinger in 1833 (as stated earlier, such a score was never produced) is actually the Kistner score (plate no. 3050) from ca 1865–8. Stegemann's claim (xvi) that 'its readings have in general been preferred' as it 'is the oldest source, and the only one that is certainly based on Chopin's autograph', thus has dire consequences. And his 'first German edition' of the 'piano arrangement', with plate no. 2340 (xii, xiii), is not the 1833 impression but Kistner's altogether new edition from ca 1858, which, as mentioned earlier, contains copious emendations.

48　See Chomiński and Turło, *Katalog*, 347–9 for details.

49　A full list appears in ibid., 347–8. See also Ekier, 'Zagadnienie', 89–90.

50　The discography in Appendix 3 derives from Kański, *Dyskografia*; James Methuen-Campbell, 'A historical survey of Chopin on disc', in Samson (ed.), *Cambridge Companion*, 284–94; Methuen-Campbell, *Chopin Playing*; and the National Sound Archive, London. Note that multiple catalogue numbers exist for some recordings, and that details vary between these sources.

51　For discussion see Chopin, *Esquisses*, and Rink, 'Authentic Chopin'; see also Methuen-Campbell, *Chopin Playing*, and Samson, *Four Ballades*, where trends in Chopin performance are more fully documented. As noted before, many of these changes in performing practice infiltrated the editions studied above.

52　Transcribed 20 April 1843 by Ferdinand Denis; quoted from Eigeldinger, *Chopin: Pianist*, 142 n. 157.

53 Quoted from Eigeldinger, *Chopin: Pianist*, 277; my emphasis.

54 See Rink, 'Translating'.

55 Koczalski inherited Chopin's performance approach from his teacher Mikuli, who studied with Chopin. See Eigeldinger, *Chopin: Pianist*, 97–8 n. 20.

56 Recall Kleczyński's advice on playing *gruppetti* (see p. 23).

57 Tan uses an Erard from 1858 – a piano post-dating Chopin's concertos by almost thirty years, and a make about which he expressed strong reservations (see Eigeldinger, *Chopin: Pianist*, 25–6, 91–2 n. 7 and 92–3 nn. 9–10).

58 Another sphere of reception history is composition. In *Instrumentalkonzert*, Engel claims that concertos (or concerto-like works) inspired by Chopin's include those of Anton Arensky (417), Gabriel Fauré (374), Simon Jadassohn (354), Ignacy Paderewski (422), Cipriani Potter (274), Ebenezer Prout (538), Anton Rubinstein (408), Alexander Skryabin (418) and Edward Wolff (368). As compositional influence extends beyond the music's own boundaries, this issue will not be addressed here.

4 Re-evaluation

1 These comments derive from John Rink, 'Le processus narratif dans l'interprétation et l'analyse', *Musurgia* 2/2 (1995), 28–9. See also Rink, 'Translating' concerning the hierarchical organisation of musical performance.

2 The main premise of Schenkerian theory is that 'masterpieces of tonal music are based on a hierarchy of interdependent structures ranging from the "fundamental structure" (*Ursatz*) and the "background" level . . . to increasingly complex elaborations or prolongations of this remote structure at "middleground" and "foreground" levels. According to Schenker, this multi-layered foundation is the principal source of unity and coherence in a work' (Rink, 'Tonal architecture', 306).

3 The ensuing analysis is based on Ekier's edition of Op. 21, Zimmermann's of Op. 11 and Brahms's orchestral parts for both concertos.

4 These repeated structures are typical of the 'dynamic', goal-directed progressions appearing in Chopin's music around this time; they achieve greater structural momentum than the generally symmetrical models previously employed (see p. 10).

5 Most performers take a much slower tempo. It is possible that Chopin miscalculated the metronome marking (perhaps late in the notation process: see Kallberg, 'Chopin', 542); but such a rapid tempo animates the music, provided that the pianist's touch is from the finger, as Chopin wanted, not from the wrist or arm, as advocated by Kalkbrenner and other contemporaries.

Slowing would naturally have occurred at cadence points and possibly in more reflective passages, although note Mikuli's insistence that 'the metronome never left [Chopin's] piano' (quoted from Eigeldinger, *Chopin: Pianist*, 49).

6 See Samson, *Music of Chopin*, 52ff.

7 Note too the horn interjection in bars 96–8 – the only instrument apart from strings to play between bar 68 and the buildup to T_2 in bars 179ff.

8 Bars 115–24 demonstrate the 'naturalness' of Chopin's keyboard technique. Although rapid, the figuration is not difficult, the second and third fingers acting as pivots between changing hand positions. (Chopin stresses the pivotal role of these fingers in his unfinished piano method; see Chopin, *Esquisses*, 74 and 78.) In bars 123–4, for instance, the wrist gently inscribes an arc guiding the hand through higher or lower registers, and while bars 115–16 are more complex in contour, they exploit the same energy-generating mechanism. Playing such passages is almost effortless, the music flowing of its own accord.

9 See Rink, 'Authentic Chopin', 235–44 for detailed analysis of this passage, which is likened to the recitative in Bach's Chromatic Fantasy. Although more profound in impact, the passage also recalls the end of the third solo in Hummel's Op. 85, first movement (see pp. 70–1).

10 This type of progression, from V^7 to (♭)VI, was savaged by Schumann as a cliché in run-of-the-mill piano concertos (review of Kalkbrenner's Concerto Op. 127, *Neue Zeitschrift für Musik* 4 (1836), 113).

11 This octave texture anticipates the Larghetto's recitative section.

12 Although more technically assured, this section recalls the passagework in Chopin's earlier pieces with orchestra.

13 Ubiquitous in the *stile brillante*, consecutive thirds are generally lyrical rather than virtuosic in Chopin's concertos, especially the slow movements.

14 Note the insistent g^1–f^1 tenor appoggiaturas in bars 294–6; also the bass ascent through an octave in bars 296–300, articulated by the cello and, at times, the piano.

15 This point echoes Samson, *Master Musicians*, 48. Recall that the *Powszechny dziennik krajowy* (19 March 1830) discerned an 'imperceptible' blend of tutti and solo sections, while the *Kurier polski* (20 March) praised Chopin for moulding melodic and virtuosic passages 'into a unified whole'.

16 The second movement of Dobrzyński's Concerto in A♭ major Op. 2 may also have been influenced by Moscheles' Op. 58: like Op. 21, it features a recitative in its middle section. Although dated 1824 by Dobrzyński himself, the concerto could have been composed after he and Chopin became colleagues at the Szkoła Główna Muzyki in 1826. (See Baculewski, 'Zawikłane', 5.)

17 This recitative sounds astonishingly wooden in many recordings, the *fiori-ture* parsed into fractionally equivalent units. Compare the reaction of the *Powszechny dziennik krajowy* of 4 March 1830 to Chopin's performance the previous day: 'The Adagio, usually a tiresome part of any piano concerto, delighted everyone, especially in the passage where the whole orchestra played a *tremolando* while the soloist executed a recitative of rich tonal diversity' (translation from Atwood, *Chopin*, 206). This alternation between slow appoggiaturas and fast flourishes may derive from the baroque improvisatory tradition embodied in Bach's Chromatic Fantasy (see n. 9 above).

18 See Chapter 3, n. 28. The bass plays pizzicato except in bars 62–6^1. Other additions to the tremolo backdrop (played by the remaining strings) include the cadential punctuation of flutes and clarinets in bars 59–60 and 61–2. Ekier's and Zimmermann's editions of Op. 21 reproduce the alternative accompaniment written into Stirling's score for use in solo performance (see p. 23).

19 The unity of bars 72–4 prompted Brahms to amalgamate them into one bar in his Breitkopf edition.

20 The partial autograph and first editions differ in pitch material here and in bar 81.

21 Perhaps referring to Chopin's letter of 20 October 1829 to Tytus (see p. 12), Tovey drolly comments that 'for reasons unknown to history', the composer called this movement a rondo ('Chopin. Pianoforte Concerto in F minor', in *Essays*, 106). In fact, it is not thus labelled. Compare the third movement of Dobrzyński's Concerto, which, according to Baculewski ('Zawikłane', 5), derives from sonata and variation forms, having a ternary construction.

22 As we shall see, episode 2 successively treats themes 2b (bars 245ff.), 2d (bars 257ff.), 2a and 2c (bars 261ff.), 2a (bars 293ff.), and 1 (bars 309ff.). 2d is also developed in section A' (bars 353ff.).

23 The *Kurier warszawski* of 18 March 1830 commented on the 'extremely charming variations' of 'the mazurka in this Rondo' (translation from Atwood, *Chopin*, 208).

24 The mazurka genre thus fostered both Chopin's 'organic' technique and his unique phraseology – typically based on four- or eight-bar units, like the dance, but subtly altered to enhance the music's innate momentum. Despite the mazurka's influence, Chopin instructed Dubois to play the anacrustic arpeggio in bar 27 on the beat, in eighteenth-century style, even though – or because – this distorts the first beat's rhythm.

25 Compare the introductions in Chopin's Mazurkas Op. 6 No. 3 and Op. 68 No. 3, trio section. Abraham ('Chopin', 86) proposes that Chopin borrowed the 'col legno' articulation from Kurpiński's opera *Nowe Krakowiaki*.

26 For instance, compare the kujawiak in Op. 13 and the second themes in Op. 14 and Op. 11, Rondo.

27 Compare the retransition in the Scherzo Op. 31 (bars 560–83).

28 See Abraham, *Chopin's Musical Style*, 18–19; compare bars 285–90, which anticipate this descent. Such devices cloud the music before points of structural articulation, making these seem especially transparent.

29 Marked 'Cor de signal' in the first editions but not in Chopin's partial autograph, this is often compared to the solo horn obbligato in the rondo of Weber's Concerto Op. 32, bars 293–301.

30 An analogous tonal scheme is used in Chopin's C♯minor Scherzo Op. 39 (see Rink, 'Authentic Chopin', 217–26).

31 The presence of two themes within the first group – acting respectively as 'announcement' and 'principal subject' – echoes Hummel Opp. 85 and 89, Kalkbrenner Op. 61, Moscheles Op. 58, and of course Chopin Op. 21. In addition, Op. 11's chromatic descent in the bass, subdued lead-in to the piano's entrance and pulsating accompanimental rhythms correspond to various of these models (as does the 'Allegro maestoso' indication, used by Kalkbrenner).

32 The ascending arpeggios in bars 141 and 149 should be treated as 'rhythmic crescendos', with progressively shorter durations accelerating towards the peak, rather than pedantically counted as in many recordings. In Dubois, diagonal lines are indicated before the last note in bar 141 and after the cadence in bar 146 – respectively to change hand position and to mark the *Eingang*'s phrase division.

33 Although similar to bars 92–100 in Kalkbrenner's Op. 61, Chopin's *Eingang* is vastly superior in design. Mikuli reports a variant for bar 153, beat 2 (shown in Henle, 110; see Chapter 2, n. 45).

34 For all its surface complexity, the melody is based on a simple 'skeleton':

bar:	155	158	161	162	170		171	174	175		178	179
principal pitch:	B →A		→	G →F♯		‖	B → A		→		G → F♯→E	
harmonic support:	i	ii⁷	V⁷	i	V		i	iv⁶₄	V⁶₅	i	V	i

35 Recall Lenz's remark (quoted on p. 24) that Chopin 'wanted the runs *cantabile*', 'thematic fragments' brought out as much as possible, 'using the most delicate touch'.

36 The octaves should be regarded as two parallel voices, rather than as timbral reinforcement – a stylistic feature distinguishing Chopin from his contemporaries (but cf. pp. 96–8).

37 This juxtaposition can be awkward in performance – hence the jarring effect in many recordings. Chopin's '*p*', 'leggierissimo' and 'poco crescendo' should be strictly observed.

38 Compare the acciaccatura-laden descent in Hummel's Op. 85, Allegro moderato, bar 163. Although similar, Chopin's is more expressively integrated; it is also pianistically 'natural', the second and fourth fingers folding over the thumb as the hand passes down the keyboard. Samson (*Music of Chopin*, 54) comments: 'It was common practice for the second ritornello to give way to . . . a ruminative solo (Weber C major, Hummel A minor, Field A♭ major and Kalkbrenner D minor), but Chopin's melody breathes a fresher air, uniquely his own.'

39 On the downbeat of bar 416, the French first edition specifies b^1 in the piano's treble, in keeping with the first violin, resolution occurring within beat 2. The Kistner edition, however, wrongly 'corrects' this to a^1 (presumably without reference to the orchestral accompaniment), thereby creating a clash. Astonishingly, modern editions like Zimmermann's and Stegemann's perpetuate the error.

40 Other material from T_1 reappears later in T_4, thus integrating the orchestral passages. Incidentally, the cuts in many early recordings make T_1 and T_3 identical, thus stultifying the momentum created by the latter's composed abbreviation.

41 Compare the first section of Chopin's F major Nocturne Op. 15 No. 1, discussed in Rink, 'Evolution', 169.

42 Eigeldinger ('Placing Chopin', 129) likens the kaleidoscopic colours to a glass harmonica.

43 In Op. 5 and Op. 16, the formal succession is in fact A–B–A–B–A', the last part being extended in preparation for the 'finale'. Op. 16 also contains an introduction.

44 Greater integration is also achieved in the *Rondo à la krakowiak* Op. 14 (see p. 9), which in many respects resembles this movement – thematic construction, phraseology, rhythm and orchestral deployment – although the key scheme differs.

45 Compare Chopin's polonaise for piano and orchestra, published as Op. 22 – a counterpart to the mazurka- and krakowiak-inspired movements in Op. 21 and Op. 11.

46 Note the $\hat{6} \rightarrow \hat{5}$ motions in bars 233, 235, 237 and 239. (As observed on p. 32, $c\sharp^3$ should appear in bars 233 and 235, not $c\natural^3$ as in most editions.)

47 Abraham (*Chopin's Musical Style*, 34) calls this a 'touch of humour almost worthy of Beethoven'. It might have been inspired by the third movement of Hummel's E major Concerto Op. 110 (published in 1826), which also contains a thematic reprise in E♭ major, just before the 'finale'.

48 As stated on pp. 37–8, Balakirev's reorchestration embellishes the arpeggios with developmental thematic reminiscences.

49 See Abraham, 'Chopin'; Ekier, 'Zagadnienie'; Aleksander Frączkiewicz, 'Instrumentacja koncertów Chopina', *Muzyka* 3/3–4 (1952), 75–82; Zieliński, *Chopin*, 169–70 and 223–4; and Zimmermann, 'Chopin'. See also Stefan Sledziński, 'Na temat domniemanego udziału I. F. Dobrzyńskiego w instrumentacji koncertów Chopina', *Muzyka* 6/1–2 (1955), 16–31 regarding Dobrzyński's putative confession to Adam Münchheimer (reported by Ferdynand Hoesick) that he had completed the instrumentation of both concertos for Chopin – a claim that can be rejected outright. (See Chapter 2, n. 7.)

50 This may be why Chopin appears to have played with orchestral or chamber accompaniment in all of the public performances cited in Chapter 2, although the hand-written accompaniment in Stirling's score of the Larghetto indicates that he must have envisaged solo renditions of at least the slow movements.

5 Chopin's third concerto

1 Samson, *Music of Chopin*, 192.

2 Published by Schlesinger (plate no. 3208) and dedicated 'à son ami Frédéric Chopin', Wolff's *Grand allegro* corresponds to the opening movement of his first concerto; its most interesting feature is the use of a cadenza to herald S_1, as in Op. 46. The epigonic Wolff may have 'stolen' Chopin's title in advance – hence the latter's warning to Fontana in his letter of 20 October 1841 (quoted in n. 16 below).

3 Compare also Alkan's 'Tutti de Concerto dans le genre ancien', in *Esquisses: 48 Motifs* (1861). For discussion of the expanding rift between soloist and orchestra in 1830s piano concertos, see Robert Schumann, 'Das Clavier-Concert', *Neue Zeitschrift für Musik* 10 (1839), 5–7.

4 See his letter of June 1841 to Julian Fontana, in *Korespondencja*, II:21; see also Jeffrey Kallberg, 'Chopin's last style', *Journal of the American Musicological Society* 38 (1985), 264–315.

5 Chopin, *Selected Correspondence*, 71.

6 Ibid., 122. Most of Chopin's own letters from 1833 and early 1834 have not survived.

7 Ibid., 126.

8 See Wilhelm Hitzig, ' "Pariser Briefe". Ein Beitrag zur Arbeit des deutschen Musikverlags aus den Jahren 1833–1840', *Der Bär. Jahrbuch von Breitkopf & Härtel auf die Jahre 1929/1930* (Leipzig 1930), 41, 43.

9 Kallberg, 'Chopin', 803.

10 According to Berlioz (*Le Rénovateur*, 23 February 1834), the concerto

'sparkled with brilliance, grace, freshness, striking whims and fancies, delicate figurations and ravishing arabesques, executed with the superior talent
for which he is known' (see Chapter 2, n. 14).

11 'Madame Streicher's . . . recollections of Chopin, based on extracts from her
carefully-kept diary of the years 1839, 1840, and 1841', in Niecks, *Chopin*,
II:343. Müller's wording could of course indicate either an entirely new
composition or one recycled from older material. The term used in the
German version of Niecks – 'Concertstück' – may be Müller's own (see
Eigeldinger, *Chopin: Pianist*, 182–3). Müller was a professional pianist until
her marriage to J. B. Streicher in 1849. The reference to her as a 'cherished
disciple' is Marmontel's; see Niecks, *Chopin*, II:176.

12 Chopin, *Selected Correspondence*, 194.

13 This three-page letter was auctioned at Drouot-Richelieu, Paris, on 30 April
1997, as part of the Barbier and Mongrédien collections. In the letter (sent
from 5 rue Tronchet, Paris) Chopin also offers Breitkopf & Härtel Op. 47,
Op. 48 and Op. 49 for 500 francs each, asking for the publisher's agreement
to these terms. I am grateful to Jeffrey Kallberg for informing me of the
letter, and to Jean-Jacques Eigeldinger and Christophe Grabowski for providing copies.

14 Chopin, *Selected Correspondence*, 209. Until now, this wording has been
explained in terms of Op. 46's concerto–like qualities, not its compositional
genesis.

15 Chopin adds: 'The same for the Fantasia [Op. 49]: at least 500. However, I
will let him have the Nocturnes [Op. 48], the Ballade [Op. 47] and the Polonaise [Op. 44] for 300 each' (ibid., 209). Masset was the business partner of
Troupenas, one of Chopin's French publishers.

16 Ibid., 211. The letter continues: 'Don't show it to Wolff for he always grabs
something and prints it before time, and don't trust his friend Meissonnier
or anything connected with him'.

17 *Korespondencja*, II:48. The title and first pages of Op. 46's manuscript are
reproduced in Tomaszewski and Weber, *Chopin*, 183.

18 For details of the corrections see the Critical Report in Henle's *Klavierstücke*
volume. According to Christophe Grabowski ('Les Editions originales
françaises des œuvres de Frédéric Chopin', *Revue de musicologie* 82 (1996),
242), the second impression – also from 1841 – has a modified title page. It is
likely that Chopin deliberately changed the time signature from ¢ to C
when correcting the proofs – hence its retention in the later impression.

19 These publication details come from Chomiński and Turło, *Katalog*, 70.

20 Szulc, *Fryderyk Chopin i utwory jego muzyczne* (Poznań 1873), 81. Tomaszewski and Weber (*Chopin*, 183) note that Chopin's words were recorded by

Hoffmann's wife, Emilia Borzęcka. Chopin sent Hoffmann a copy of the *Allegro de concert* with the dedication: 'To the Silesian craftsman – from the ordinary player' (translation from Franciszek German, 'Chopin relics in Upper Silesia', in *Chopin in Silesia*, tr. Czesław Boniakowski (Katowice 1974), 16).

21 Müller states: 'The promised concert-piece, Op. 46, had to my inexpressible delight been published [by then]. I played it to him, and he was satisfied with my playing of it'. Quoted from Niecks, *Chopin*, II:343.

22 Compare the abbreviated tuttis in certain recordings of Op. 11 (although the cut here is in a solo work). The deletion – which surely reflects an original orchestral conception – was specified in a private communication from Jean-Jacques Eigeldinger (whose *Chopin: Pianist* (213 n. 30) states that it extends to bar 83). Eigeldinger also confirms that a cross appears at the beginning of bar 12, above the upper system (as in Stirling's scores of the Etude Op. 10 No. 3 and Mazurka Op. 33 No. 4); the deleted passage is struck through in pencil. I am grateful to Eigeldinger for this information and for generously sharing his transcription of Franchomme's score (see below).

23 They include minor typographical corrections in bars 97 and 127.

24 Bourges, 'Lettres à Mme la Baronne de ***', *Revue et Gazette musicale de Paris* 9 (1842), 172.

25 Schumann, 'Pianofortemusik', *Neue Zeitschrift für Musik* 17 (1842), 168.

26 Niecks, *Chopin*, II:223, 224. He does however cite a review in the *Athenaeum*, 21 January 1888, stating that although Op. 46 'is generally regarded as one of Chopin's least interesting and least characteristic pieces', 'these impressions are distinctly wrong', particularly in the performance of Vladimir de Pachmann – 'an astounding revelation', 'nothing short of an artistic creation' (ibid., II:224–5 n. 9).

27 Huneker, *Chopin*, 176.

28 Ashton Jonson, *A Handbook to Chopin's Works* (London 1905), 146, 147.

29 Leichtentritt, *Chopin*, 91. Compare Zieliński, *Chopin*, 628–9.

30 Weissmann, *Chopin*, 173.

31 Scharlitt, *Chopin*, 276.

32 Jachimecki, *Chopin*, 207.

33 Cortot, *In Search*, 58. Nicodé's orchestration is discussed below.

34 Jachimecki, *Chopin*, 206; Weinstock, *Chopin*, 254.

35 Furthermore: 'There is certainly an advance in some respects on the two concertos, but the thematic material was clearly conceived at the earlier date [i.e. early 1830s], if indeed not before'. Gould, 'Sonatas', 155–6, 157. Hedley (*Chopin*, 140) similarly asserts: 'The themes do not represent the Chopin of 1841, although certain portions of the work belong to his later style.'

36 Samson, *Master Musicians*, 213.

37 Samson, *Music of Chopin*, 56–7.

38 These date from the 1880s. Op. 46's various transcriptions are detailed in Chomiński and Turło, *Katalog*, 338.

39 As of 1949 the work had 'never been recorded' (according to Armand Panigel, *L'œuvre de Frédéric Chopin: discographie générale* (Paris 1949), 25), and only a handful of recordings are cited in Kański, *Dyskografia*, and Methuen-Campbell, *Chopin Playing*. Others in addition to those discussed below include Hamish Milne's (CRD 1060, from 1981) and Michel Dussault's (Musica Viva MVCD 1045, from 1992). Ponti's recording, conducted by Volker Schmidt-Gertenbach, dates from 1978.

40 Compare for instance the overture of Auber's *La Muette de Portici*, an opera known to Chopin (see p. 7). Its D major theme at bars 143ff., later expanded in G major, shares many features with both the opening of Op. 46 and, in particular, the second theme in bars 41ff., including a strong processional impulse and cadential 'punctuation'. Meyerbeer's *Robert le diable* – a source of inspiration to Chopin in various works from the early to mid 1830s (see Gerhard, 'Ballade') – also contains second-beat punctuation (e.g. overture, bars 9 and 14) as well as the 'timpani' rhythm found in bars 38–9 *et seq.* of Op. 46 (overture, bars 23ff.). Compare too the opening sections in Chopin's Fantasy Op. 49. Unlike the concertos, Op. 46 lacks a metronome marking, Chopin having ceased to specify these in the mid 1830s.

41 Compare the cadenza in Chopin's Nocturne Op. 9 No. 2, composed ca 1830–2. The triple trills in bar 89 and later anticipate those in the Polonaise-Fantasy Op. 61 (1845–6).

42 Note also the unusual trill notation in bars 130 and 206, whereby the trill begins not on the upper or lower auxiliary but, exceptionally, on the principal pitch (see Eigeldinger, *Chopin: Pianist*, 131 n. 126; cf. however bars 53, 136 and 212).

43 These rapid harmonic juxtapositions recall certain progressions in the Warsaw-period music, but here they have motivic significance while fragmenting the phrase structure in advance of the lengthy prolongation of V of V to follow.

44 Compare bars 62–70 of the Barcarolle Op. 60 (1845–6), also in A major.

45 Recall Lenz's words: 'to play the [first] movement right through . . . would affect Chopin too powerfully'. See also Chapter 2, n. 52.

46 See Chapter 2, n. 15. Jean-Jacques Eigeldinger has commented in private correspondence that this incompatibility may have extended to Chopin's idiosyncratic rubato – possibly one reason why he declined to play with orchestra in London in 1848, when only one rehearsal would have been pos-

sible. (See his letter of 13 May 1848 to Wojciech Grzymała in Paris, in *Selected Correspondence*, 316.)

47 See Samson, *Master Musicians*, 213. Comparison with another contemporaneous work in A major, the Polonaise Op. 40 No. 1 ('Military'), is instructive. Samson (ibid., 154) writes that the Polonaise projects 'both an image of the old Poland, warlike and chivalrous, and at the same time a call to arms for the new Poland, and it is perhaps the one piece of Chopin which might justify Schumann's reference to "concealed guns"'. Although more heroic than martial, Op. 46 also conveys this double image.

Select bibliography

Abraham, Gerald. 'Chopin and the orchestra', in Lissa (ed.), *Book*, 85–7
    Chopin's Musical Style (London 1939)

Amster, Isabella. *Das Virtuosenkonzert in der ersten Hälfte des 19. Jahrhunderts*
    (Wolfenbüttel and Berlin [1931])

Atwood, William G. *Fryderyk Chopin: Pianist from Warsaw* (New York 1987)

Baculewski, Krzysztof. 'Zawikłane dzieje koncertu fortepianowego Ignacego
    Feliksa Dobrzyńskiego', *Ruch muzyczny* 33/5 (1989), 3–7

Bloom, Peter (ed.). *Music in Paris in the Eighteen-thirties* (Stuyvesant, New York
    1987)

Chechlińska, Zofia. 'The National Edition of Chopin's works', *Chopin Studies* 2
    (1987), 7–19

Chomiński, Józef Michał. *Fryderyk Chopin*, tr. Bolko Schweinitz (Leipzig 1980)

Chomiński, Józef Michał and Teresa Dalila Turło. *Katalog dzieł Fryderyka
    Chopina* (Cracow and Warsaw 1990)

Chopin, Fryderyk. *Esquisses pour une Méthode de Piano*, coll. and ed. Jean-
    Jacques Eigeldinger (Paris 1993)

    Korespondencja Fryderyka Chopina, ed. Bronisław Edward Sydow, 2 vols.
    (Warsaw 1955)

    Selected Correspondence of Fryderyk Chopin, tr. and ed. Arthur Hedley
    (London 1962)

Cortot, Alfred. *In Search of Chopin*, tr. Cyril and Rena Clarke (London and New
    York 1951)

Dahlhaus, Carl. *Nineteenth-Century Music*, tr. J. Bradford Robinson (Berkeley
    and Los Angeles 1989)

Eigeldinger, Jean-Jacques. *Chopin: Pianist and Teacher as Seen by His Pupils*, tr.
    Naomi Shohet with Krysia Osostowicz and Roy Howat, ed. Roy Howat
    (Cambridge 1986)

    'Les premiers concerts de Chopin à Paris (1832–1838)', in Bloom (ed.), *Music
    in Paris*, 251–97

    'Placing Chopin: reflections on a compositional aesthetic', in Rink and
    Samson (eds.), *Chopin Studies 2*, 102–39

Ekier, Jan. 'Zagadnienie opracowań akompaniamentów orkiestrowych koncertów fortepianowych Fryderyka Chopina', *Muzyka* 3/3–4 (1952), 83–95

Engel, Hans. *Das Instrumentalkonzert* (Leipzig 1932)

Frączkiewicz, Aleksander. 'Koncerty fortepianowe Chopina jako typ koncertu romantycznego', in Lissa (ed.), *Book*, 293–6

Gerhard, Anselm. 'Ballade und Drama', *Archiv für Musikwissenschaft* 48 (1991), 110–25

Gould, Peter. 'Sonatas and concertos', in Alan Walker (ed.), *Frédéric Chopin: Profiles of the Man and the Musician* (London 1966), 144–69

Hedley, Arthur. *Chopin* (London 1947)

Huneker, James. *Chopin: The Man and His Music* (New York 1900)

Jachimecki, Zdislas. *Frédéric Chopin et son œuvre* (Paris 1930)

Kallberg, Jeffrey. 'Chopin in the marketplace: aspects of the international music publishing industry in the first half of the nineteenth century', *Notes* 39 (1983), 535–69, 795–824

Kański, Józef. *Dyskografia chopinowska* (Cracow 1986)

Kobylańska, Krystyna. *Rękopisy utworów Chopina: Katalog*, 2 vols. (Cracow 1977)

Kobylańska, Krystyna (coll. and ed.). *Chopin in His Own Land: Documents and Souvenirs*, tr. Claire Grece-Dąbrowska and Mary Filippi (Cracow 1955)

Leichtentritt, Hugo. *Frédéric Chopin* (Berlin 1905)

Lenz, Wilhelm von. 'Uebersichtliche Beurtheilung der Pianoforte-Kompositionen von Chopin', *Neue Berliner Musikzeitung* 26 (1872), 282–3

Lissa, Zofia (ed.). *The Book of the First International Musicological Congress Devoted to the Works of Frederick Chopin* (Warsaw 1963)

Methuen-Campbell, James. *Chopin Playing* (London 1981)

Niecks, Frederick. *Frederick Chopin as a Man and Musician*, 3rd edn, 2 vols. (London 1902; 1st edn, London 1888)

Ringer, Alexander (ed.). *The Early Romantic Era* (London 1990)

Rink, John. 'Authentic Chopin: history, analysis and intuition in performance', in Rink and Samson (eds.), *Chopin Studies 2*, 214–44

'The evolution of Chopin's "structural style" and its relation to improvisation' (Ph.D. diss., University of Cambridge 1989)

'Tonal architecture in the early music', in Samson (ed.), *Cambridge Companion*, 78–97 and 305–8

'Translating musical meaning: the nineteenth-century performer as narrator', in Nicholas Cook and Mark Everist (eds.), *Rethinking Music: Issues of Historiography* (Oxford, in press)

Rink, John and Jim Samson (eds.). *Chopin Studies 2* (Cambridge 1994)

Roeder, Michael Thomas. *A History of the Concerto* (Portland, Oregon 1994)

Sachs, Joel. 'London: the professionalization of music', in Ringer (ed.), *Early Romantic*, 201–35

Samson, Jim. 'Chopin reception: theory, history, analysis', in Rink and Samson (eds.), *Chopin Studies 2*, 1–17
  Chopin: The Four Ballades (Cambridge 1992)
  The Master Musicians: Chopin (Oxford 1996)
  The Music of Chopin (London 1985)

Samson, Jim (ed.). *The Cambridge Companion to Chopin* (Cambridge 1992)

Scharlitt, Bernard. *Chopin* (Leipzig 1919)

Schering, Arnold. *Geschichte des Instrumentalkonzerts bis auf die Gegenwart* (Wiesbaden 1927)

Schumann, Robert. 'Pianoforte. Concerte. Friedrich Chopin', *Neue Zeitschrift für Musik* 4 (1836), 137–9

Smialek, William. *Ignacy Feliks Dobrzyński and Musical Life in Nineteenth-Century Poland* (Lewiston, New York 1991)

Stevens, Jane R. 'Theme, harmony, and texture in classic-romantic descriptions of concerto first-movement form', *Journal of the American Musicological Society* 27 (1974), 25–60

Szalsza, Piotr. 'Über die Wiener Konzerte von Frédéric Chopin', *Studien zur Musikwissenschaft* 37 (1986), 27–35

Tomaszewski, Mieczysław and Bożena Weber. *Fryderyk Chopin: A Diary in Images*, tr. Rosemary Hunt (Cracow and Warsaw 1990)

Tovey, Donald Francis. *Essays in Musical Analysis, III: Concertos* (London 1936)

Weinstock, Herbert. *Chopin: The Man and His Music* (New York 1959)

Weissmann, Adolf. *Chopin* (Berlin and Leipzig 1912)

Wróblewska-Straus, Hanna. 'Manuscrits inconnus des œuvres de l'opus 21, 34, 40 et 49 de Frédéric Chopin', *Chopin Studies* 3 (1990), 131–68

Zieliński, Tadeusz A. *Frédéric Chopin*, tr. Marie Bouvard, Laurence Dyèvre, Blaise de Obaldia and Krystyna de Obaldia (Paris 1995)

Zimmermann, Ewald. 'Chopin und sein Orchester', *Chopin Studies* 3 (1990), 175–83

Index

Index